Raymond

Best wishes

Pure Luck

JB Raymond.

THE BEST OF PRUE LEITH

THE BEST OF
Prue Leith

*Prue Leith
and
Jean-Baptiste Reynaud*

J M Dent & Sons Ltd

LONDON MELBOURNE TORONTO

First published 1979
© Leith's Farm Limited 1979

Photoset by Northampton Phototypesetters Ltd
Printed in Great Britain by
Billings Ltd, London Guildford & Worcester for
J. M. Dent & Sons Ltd
Aldine House, Welbeck Street, London

This book is set in 11 on 11 pt Monophoto Baskerville

British Library Cataloguing in Publication Data

Leith, Prudence
  The best of Prue Leith.
  1. Cookery
  I. Title   II. Reynaud, Jean
  641.5   TX717

ISBN 0-460-04368-4

Contents

TO MY WIFE HEIDI AND OUR THREE
CHILDREN,
MY *impitoyable* CRITICS
JBR

and

TO SEEMAH JOSHUA FOR HER SKILLS,
HER LOYALTY AND HER FRIENDSHIP
PL

Introduction

This book started as a collection of those recipes that Jean-Baptiste and I are constantly asked for by our restaurant customers: recipes for dishes like our Chicken Breast with Ginger and Gruyère, the house version of Duck with Almonds, and the simple passion fruit syllabub for which the recipes had to be printed to keep up with demand.

But very quickly we discovered that a book of our 'favourite recipes' had to include dishes that would never sell in a fixed-price expensive restaurant. So, although the bulk of the book consists of the sort of simple but elegant food we try to make in the restaurant, a good few of the recipes turned out to be family fare like Red Bean and Onion Salad or Mushroom and Macaroni Pie. Even the super-gourmet cannot live by caviar alone. Both palate and pocketbook demand a balance of 'plain home cooking' and of festive richness.

One of the great pleasures of working with JBR (who is a chef by trade and Managing Director of Leith's Restaurant) and with Head-Chef Max Markarian, has been the stimulation of their enthusiasm and inventiveness.

My co-author is the true Frenchman. Ever a gourmet, but never a food snob, he waxes as lyrical about a hefty *cassoulet* eaten at a *relais de routiers* (motorway caff to us English unfortunates) or an *Anchoïade* bought on the beach, as about the fine Scallop Quenelles with Lobster Sauce with which he makes our customers' separation from their money positively pleasurable.

7

Maybe it is Chef Max's Armenian background that disposes him so happily to the use of coriander, ginger and nutmeg, to the judicious employment of the marinade, and the frequent use of the charcoal grill. But, thank God, his culinary inventiveness never takes him into those boggy pastures of gimmicky concoctions, blurred tastes, and lurid appearance. Not for him the slice of gammon coated with walnuts, topped with pineapple, glazed with cheese, and served with half a tomato, cut *à la zigzag*.

Really this book should have been written by the three of us, but if our three-monthly menu conferences are anything to go by we would never have stopped shouting long enough to write the book. As it is, JBR and I had a battle confining ourselves to two hundred recipes and Max, for sure, would have pushed it up by another hundred or so. But I would like him to know that we are grateful for his very real contribution.

I'd also like to thank my husband, nanny and children for putting up uncomplainingly (well, almost uncomplainingly) with sausages and frozen pizza because the mistress of the house has been too busy writing about Peppered Veal Kidney and Raspberry Malakoff to cook their dinners. If I had at least tested the recipes myself and let them be the judges of Baked Banana and Rhubarb with Rum and Burnt Sugar, etc. I'd have a clearer conscience. But JBR, Max, my friend Annie Langford, the staff and students of Leith's School of Food and Wine, and the cooks at Leith's Good Food, Caterers, did the testing between them. I am grateful for that too. It is a painstaking and maddening job, but vital to a good cook book. If a novelist or mathematician or even an historian makes mistakes in his books, the most it means is the reader has wasted his purchase money. If cookery writers make them it can mean expensive ingredients in the dustbin, and the ruination not only of the dinner but of the cook's temper too.

The recipes for this book have been carefully adapted for the home cook, and information has been included to help with the pre-preparation and possible freezing. Neither JBR nor I is entirely in love with the freezer – indeed at Leith's our freezer usually contains only raw prawns (unavailable fresh), cooked choux pastry, and the fresh herbs we grow for the restaurant and cannot get all the year round. But to ignore the usefulness of a freezer is idiotic. As a housewife I know perfectly well that sometimes my time, or my peace of mind, is more important than gastronomic perfection, and my home freezer is rather fuller than the restaurant's.

Which brings me to a word about the use of recipes. It has been my experience that only second-class chefs are too proud to use a recipe, and only bad-tempered or self-important ones refuse to part with their 'trade secrets'. Any chef with a good recipe, a good trick or kitchen tip, is only too eager to pass the knowledge on. Recipes in our restaurant are kept in the kitchen and no one is too proud to consult them.

Finally, cooking is meant to be a pleasure. This book is for people who see it as such, or suspect (rightly) that, given the knowledge, they could cook well and greatly enjoy doing so.

Prue Leith

Sauces

Classic hollandaise sauce

Hollandaise is generally thought to be tricky. But the secret is to take it slowly and not to try to do anything else at the same time. It will keep for an hour or so if left standing in a bowl of hot water.

3 tablespoons wine
  vinegar
6 peppercorns
½ bay leaf
2 egg yolks
¼ lb (110 g) butter
Lemon juice (optional)
Salt

Put the vinegar, peppercorns and bay leaf into a small saucepan and boil fast until the liquid is reduced to about a tablespoonful. Strain this into a small pudding basin or into the top of a double boiler. If using a basin, fit it over a pan of simmering water so that the bottom does not quite touch the water. Alternatively fill a roasting tin with water, putting one end of it over direct heat so that the water bubbles, and standing the basin in the other less turbulent end. Add the yolks to the reduced vinegar.

With a wooden spoon or whisk beat the wine vinegar and egg yolks until smooth and, still beating, begin to add the butter bit by bit. As the egg yolks thicken the butter will be smoothly incorporated, forming an emulsion. Care must be taken that the yolks do not get hot enough to scramble.

When the sauce is thick take it off the heat and beat it well. Taste it and add lemon juice and salt as necessary. To keep the sauce warm stand it in a bowl of hot water.

Easy hollandaise sauce

Opinions are divided about whether this is really easier than the classic method. It is certainly quicker, but care must be taken not to overheat the sauce and scramble the eggs. As will be seen, the ingredients are exactly the same as for the classic hollandaise above but the method is slightly different. It gives a less rich and more fluffy result.

3 tablespoons wine
  vinegar
6 peppercorns
½ bay leaf
2 egg yolks
¼ lb (110 g) butter, melted
Lemon juice (optional)
Salt

Put the vinegar, peppercorns and bay leaf into a small saucepan and boil fast until the liquid is reduced to a tablespoonful. Strain, return to pan. Add two tablespoons water. Then add the egg yolks and mix well.

Using a wire whisk beat the mixture until frothy. Put back over direct heat and whisk steadily until well risen and mousse-like. Still whisking vigorously, slowly add the melted butter which should be tepid or cool rather than hot. The sauce will rise in the pan, creamy and frothy. By the time all the butter is incorporated you should have a thick emulsion.

Taste and add salt and lemon juice if necessary. To keep the sauce warm stand the saucepan in a bowl of very hot water.

Choron sauce

Choron sauce is a variation of hollandaise. Add tomato purée to basic hollandaise (recipes shown on p. 13), and if liked, crushed garlic as well.

Béarnaise sauce

Béarnaise sauce is a hollandaise with the addition of chopped tarragon and chervil. It may also have a small nut of meat glaze added, or the jellied juices in the bottom of the tin after meat has been roasted.

Tomato sauce

This is a herby, very Italian-tasting tomato sauce. It freezes well, and keeps ten days or so in the refrigerator.

2 tablespoons olive oil
1 medium onion, finely
  chopped
2 lb (900 g) fresh or
  tinned tomatoes
Good pinch dried oregano
  or marjoram, or 4 or 5
  sprigs fresh marjoram
3 or 4 sprigs fresh thyme
1 clove garlic, crushed
1 teaspoon sugar
Salt, freshly ground black
  pepper
¼ pint (150 ml) chicken
  stock

Heat the oil in a medium-sized saucepan with a good lid. Gently cook the chopped onion until soft and transparent. Add the rest of the ingredients and simmer gently for three-quarters of an hour, or until the sauce has a syrupy consistency.

For a more elegant and less peasant-looking sauce push the mixture through a sieve and reheat.

Basic French dressing or vinaigrette

This keeps well in the fridge, but don't add garlic, herbs or other flavourings until you need the dressing – they would lose their freshness.

3 tablespoons salad oil
1 tablespoon olive oil
1 tablespoon wine
  vinegar

Put the oils and vinegar into a screw-top jar and season well with salt and pepper. Shake the jar vigorously before pouring over your salad.

Salt, freshly ground black
  pepper

14

Mayonnaise

To succeed with mayonnaise you must make it slowly. If you add the oil too fast the whole lot curdles into an unsightly mess and you need to start again. If it *does* curdle don't throw the curdled mixture away but mix another egg yolk in the bottom of a second bowl and add the curdled mixture to it slowly, beating all the time.

2 egg yolks
1 level teaspoon made English mustard
½ teaspoon salt
¼ teaspoon white pepper
2 or 3 tablespoons wine vinegar
About ½ pint (290 ml) oil (olive oil or salad oil or a mixture)

Mix the egg yolks and the salt, pepper and mustard together in a small bowl, using a wooden spoon. Put the oil into a jug with a good lip and pour a drip or two into the egg mixture. Mix well. Then add another drip. Mix well again. Then some more oil and keep mixing. With each addition of oil you must beat enough to ensure that it is smoothly incorporated before proceeding. As the mixture thickens you may get bolder, adding thin streams of oil rather than drops. The whole process will take about ten minutes.

When you have added all the oil, or as much as you want to (you can add oil almost indefinitely but the mayonnaise becomes milder and blander in taste as you proceed) and you have a good thick emulsion, beat in the vinegar. For a sharp mayonnaise add three tablespoons, for a milder one two will be enough.

Butters

Garlic butter

Don't freeze this: the garlic gives the butter a rancid flavour after a few weeks, and other things in the freezer get tainted.

3 cloves garlic, crushed
3 oz (85 g) butter
Squeeze lemon juice
Salt, pepper

Beat the softened butter into the crushed garlic. Add the lemon juice and salt and pepper. Chill as for Roquefort butter (recipe below).

Parsley butter

3 oz (85 g) butter
2 tablespoons chopped parsley
Salt, pepper

Beat the softened butter, chopped parsley, a little salt and a good twist or two from the peppermill together. It will freeze well wrapped in greaseproof paper, plastic film or foil. If frozen in a sausage shape round slices can be cut from it to serve with fish or lamb cutlets.

Roquefort butter

3 oz (85 g) butter
3 oz (85 g) Roquefort cheese
Squeeze lemon
Salt, pepper

Combine the ingredients and put in a refrigerator to chill well. If liked the Roquefort butter can be rolled up in a piece of foil or greaseproof paper in a cylinder shape and frozen or well chilled. Round slices can then be cut from the block and served with steak.

Maître d'hôtel butter

This is parsley butter with the addition of a very finely chopped shallot, and a squeeze of lemon. It freezes well. Keeps two days in the refrigerator.

Stilton butter

Freezes well. Keeps three weeks in the refrigerator. Proceed exactly as for Roquefort butter above, using Stilton instead of Roquefort.

Mustard butter

Freezes well. Keeps three weeks in the refrigerator. Mix strong French mustard and butter in equal quantities and chill as for Roquefort butter (recipe above).

Herb butter

Freezes well. Keeps two days in the refrigerator. Flavour softened butter very strongly with any finely chopped fresh herb of your choice. Parsley and tarragon are fairly mild-tasting and about three tablespoons would be necessary to flavour 3 oz (85 g) of butter. Marjoram, thyme, fennel and dill are more strongly flavoured and one tablespoon for 3 oz (85 g) of butter would be about right. Chill as for Roquefort butter (recipe p. 19).

If the butter is to be served with fish add a good squeeze of lemon when mixing.

Vegetables

We have not included in this book many vegetable recipes apart from those which come in the first course and in the salad chapters. This is because we believe that the more simply vegetables are cooked (especially if they are to accompany main courses) the better. Really fresh vegetables need the minimum of messing about. Ideally they should be cooked at the last minute, then perhaps lightly buttered. As a rule it is better to under-cook rather than over-cook, but in recent years under-cooking vegetables has become such an obsession that many of them are now served entirely raw. This may be fine for things like peas or cauliflower which taste good raw anyway, but many vegetables such as broad beans and leeks need a little more than simple heating up to bring out the flavour.

Over-buttering is a problem too. Splashing butter all over everything can swamp the taste and spoil the texture of the vegetables. They should be lightly painted with a pastry brush dipped in melted butter.

Of course there are classic herb and vegetable combinations which it would be madness not to take advantage of. There are few things nicer than chopped fresh basil on baked tomatoes, or thyme with buttered broad beans, or a little cummin in the cabbage or caraway on the cauliflower. A vegetable flavoured with a single herb is generally nicer than one covered with a great handful of mixed herbs. Also, no herbs at all is generally better than any out of a packet.

When the summer vegetables have been around a long time, and one is frankly bored with them or the vegetables available are not at their youthful best, then it's time to ginger them up a bit: put fried chopped onions in peas, or finely diced, crisply fried bacon with the beans, or chopped hard-boiled eggs and parsley with a squeeze of lemon on the cauliflower. Add a dusting of powdered ginger and a pinch of sugar to the buttered carrots, fill the tomatoes with a garlicky pea purée, or mix the mash half and half with parsnip, celeriac or pumpkin.

Finally: one simple fresh vegetable is a lot easier and nicer to cook, serve and eat than a Covent Garden medley.

Cold Starters & Supper Dishes

Iced Soups

Iced borscht with cummin

The taste of cummin in this soup is wonderful. The soup freezes perfectly, or can be made two to three days in advance and kept chilled.

1 oz (30 g) butter
1 large onion, sliced
½ lb (225 g) raw potatoes, peeled and sliced
1 chicken stock cube
1 pint (570 ml) milk
1 large bunch parsley
Seasoning: ½ teaspoon salt, few twists freshly ground black pepper, pinch cummin powder, pinch ground cloves, pinch sugar, grated nutmeg
1 pint (570 ml) water
3–4 raw beetroots (weighing about 1 lb (450 g))
½ pint (290 ml) single cream
Lemon juice
1 carton soured cream (¼ pint (150 ml))

To serve:
1 tablespoon chopped chives

Serves 6

Melt the butter and add the sliced onion. Cook slowly until the onion is soft and beginning to colour. Add the potatoes and cook for five more minutes, slowly. Add the stock cube, the milk, parsley and seasonings. Simmer for twenty minutes.

Simmer the beets in the water with a large pinch of salt, until they are tender. Lift them out, peel them, then liquidize them with their cooking liquid.

Liquidize or sieve the milk and potato mixture, and mix with the beetroot. Add the cream. Taste, and add sufficient lemon juice to give a bite to the soup, and add more salt and pepper if necessary. Pour into individual serving dishes.

Spoon a good dollop of soured cream onto each serving. Sprinkle with chopped chives. Chill well.

Leith's gazpacho

This soup is made almost entirely in a blender but can of course be laboriously chopped and sieved by hand.
Gazpacho made with a machine is a very quick business. Gazpacho made by hand is a real labour of love. It can be successfully frozen as far as flavour goes, but the colour of the soup is impaired by this, and it is best made on the day of serving. It ferments easily in hot weather so should be kept refrigerated.

The ingredients listed below under the heading 'To serve' are *in addition to* those for the soup. So add them together when making a shopping list.

Peel the garlic, onion and cucumber. Chop into pieces small enough to go through the hole in the liquidizer top. Put the bread, garlic and egg yolk into the liquidizer and turn the machine on for a few seconds. When you have a smooth paste pour the oil in, with the machine going, in a thin steady stream. You should now have a mayonnaise-like emulsion. Add the vinegar and the onion. Liquidize until smooth. Tip into a bowl.

Now liquidize all the remaining ingredients, using the fresh and tinned tomatoes to keep the mixture liquid enough to prevent the machine clogging. Add to the mixture in the bowl, stir well, taste for seasoning, then put in the refrigerator to chill. (If a velvet-smooth soup is required it should be pushed through a fine-gauge sieve.)

If the soup is preferred thinner dilute it with iced water or tomato juice.

Serve icy-cold with the small bowls of chopped vegetables and fried croûtons handed separately.

1 thick slice white bread without the crust
1 tablespoon tarragon vinegar
6 tablespoons olive oil
1 egg yolk
2 large cloves garlic
1 lb (450 g) fresh, very ripe tomatoes
2 lb (900 g) tin Italian peeled tomatoes
2 red peppers
1 medium mild-tasting Spanish onion
½ cucumber
Plenty of salt (preferably sea salt)
Freshly ground black pepper
1 tablespoon tomato purée

To serve:
1 small bowl diced cucumber
1 small bowl green and red pepper mixed
1 small bowl diced tomatoes (skinned first)
1 small bowl chopped raw Spanish onion
1 large bowl small fried croûtons

Serves 6

Iced Polish duck and beetroot soup

This soup is light but sustaining, and can be served hot if preferred. Ideally the basic stock should be the liquor left after boiling a joint of beef, and the pieces of duck should have been recently roasted, but these left-overs are rare in a home kitchen. This modern version assumes the soup is to be made the day after a dinner of roast duck when the duck carcass will be used for the stock: boil the broken bones in 2 pints (1.15 l) of water, with a few sprigs of marjoram, a bay leaf, a sprig of thyme, a bunch of parsley and a slice or two of onion. If, after an hour, the liquid is not strongly flavoured, add two stock cubes. But don't use straight 'packet stock'. It needs the real beef or duck flavour.

Gently cook all the vegetables except the beetroot in the duck or beef dripping. Strain on the stock and simmer gently until the vegetables are cooked (about twenty minutes). Add the beetroot and simmer for ten more minutes, when the stock will have turned a lovely deep red. Skim off any fat and check the seasoning. Add the fine pieces of duck and beef. Allow to cool, then chill well. Offer the sour cream separately.

4 tablespoons small shreds cooked lean duck and/or lean beef
2 pints (1.15 l) well-seasoned stock (beef, duck or chicken)
1 tablespoon duck fat or dripping
10 oz (285 g) very finely shredded cabbage (red, green or white)
½ small leek, finely shredded
½ stick celery, finely shredded
1 small onion, chopped
6 oz (170 g) cooked beetroot, cut in matchstick shreds

To serve:
4 tablespoons sour cream

Serves 4–6

Salads

Red bean and onion salad

This is one of the few salads which can be made quite successfully two days in advance of eating. Keep refrigerated, however, as dried pulses are inclined to ferment. A dollop of sour cream on top of the salad looks and tastes good.

2 handfuls dried red
  kidney beans
1 mild Spanish onion,
  finely sliced
1 clove garlic, crushed
  (optional)
4 tablespoons French
  dressing (recipe p. 14)
Pinch dry English mustard
1 tablespoon chopped
  chives
Salt, freshly ground
  black pepper

To serve:
Sour cream (optional)

Serves 6–8

Soak the beans in cold water for at least five hours. Put them with enough fresh water to just cover them into a casserole with a lid. Bake them in a very low oven (150°C/300°F/ Gas Mark 2) until the beans are soft. This should take about three hours. When the beans are done tip them and any remaining liquid into a serving dish. Fork in the finely sliced onion.

Mix together the garlic, if used, French dressing, mustard, chopped chives, and plenty of salt and pepper, and pour over the bean and onion mixture. Taste and add more seasoning if necessary. Chill well before serving, with or without the sour cream on top.

Bean salad with pine nuts

The beans can be cooked a few hours in advance but the dressing should not be on them for more than half an hour or so before serving.

½ lb (225 g) very small French beans, cooked
½ lb (225 g) broad beans, cooked
2 oz (55 g) pine kernels (available at Greek or Italian delicatessens)
4 tablespoons French dressing (recipe p. 14)
1 teaspoon of fresh chopped marjoram or thyme

Serves 4

Remove the outer skins from the cooked broad beans and discard. Put the cooked French beans in a shallow serving dish and scatter over the peeled broad beans and the pine nuts. Mix the French dressing with the fresh thyme or marjoram and spoon all over the salad. Chill well before serving.

Cucumber with curry mayonnaise

May be prepared well in advance, and kept refrigerated until served.

1 large cucumber
3 tablespoons thick mayonnaise
3 tablespoons single cream
1 small onion, finely chopped
1 tablespoon olive oil
1 teaspoon curry powder
½ teaspoon sugar
1 teaspoon finely chopped fresh mint
Salt, pepper

Serves 4–6

Peel the cucumber and slice it as finely as possible. (If it is a large cucumber with rather coarse seeds it might be a good idea to de-seed it: to do this split the cucumber lengthways and using a melon baller or spoon scrape right down the centre of the two cucumber pieces, scraping out the seeds and discarding them.) Put the sliced cucumber into a bowl, add a dessertspoon of salt and mix well. Leave to stand for at least half an hour.

Meanwhile make the sauce. Soften the chopped onion in the oil over gentle heat. When the onion is transparent and cooked add the curry powder and stir gently for a minute or so. Allow to cool. Mix together the mayonnaise, the cream, the contents of the frying pan, the sugar and the chopped mint. Season with salt and pepper as needed.

Rinse and drain the cucumber slices and dry them well on absorbent kitchen paper or a clean tea towel. Once dry combine them with the sauce and tip into a clean serving dish.

Cucumber and mushroom salad

Do not make this more than a few hours in advance. It will not freeze.

1 cucumber, peeled
1½ oz (45 g) butter
½ lb (225 g) white button mushrooms, sliced
1 teaspoon flour
5 tablespoons good chicken stock
5 tablespoons cream
A little salt, freshly ground black pepper
1 tablespoon freshly chopped dill leaves
Squeeze lemon juice

Serves 4

Cut the cucumber into little blocks and dunk it in boiling water for five minutes. Then rinse under cold water and leave to dry completely.

Melt the butter in a shallow pan and fry the mushrooms, roughly sliced, for two or three minutes. Put in the cucumber and toss over the heat for a further minute or two or until the cucumber feels almost, but not quite, soft. Stir in the flour and add the chicken stock. Bring to the boil while stirring and simmer for two more minutes.

Remove from the heat and stir in the cream, chopped dill, salt and pepper and enough lemon juice to flavour slightly. Tip the mixture into a serving dish and keep covered until cold.

Cucumber with yogurt and mint

This salad can be made about six hours in advance and kept refrigerated until needed.

1 large cucumber
2 tablespoons salad oil
1 dessertspoon red wine vinegar
1 tablespoon finely chopped fresh mint
¼ teaspoon sugar
Salt
4 or 5 twists of the black pepper mill
1 small carton plain yogurt
½ clove garlic, finely crushed

To serve:
4 mint leaves for decoration (optional)

Serves 4

Peel the cucumber and slice it as thinly as possible, preferably on a mandolin or slicing machine. Put the cucumber slices in a bowl and sprinkle on a dessertspoon of salt. Mix well and leave for half an hour.

In the meantime mix together the oil, vinegar, sugar, chopped mint and a little salt and plenty of pepper to make the dressing.

Rinse the cucumber slices well, then dry them on absorbent paper or a clean tea towel. Toss them into the dressing, then divide into four portions, dishing them neatly onto four dessert-size plates.

Mix together the garlic and yogurt, and enough salt and pepper to season mildly. Spoon a blob of yogurt onto the top of each cucumber portion. Add a mint leaf to each dish and chill before serving.

Cherry tomato salad

This salad benefits from a good four or five hours in its dressing. It can be made at the last minute and will taste very good but is, I think, better for a little marinading.

½ lb (225 g) cherry tomatoes (the tiny ones, no bigger than a marble)
½ lb (225 g) raw peeled prawns or frozen scampi
½ lb (225 g) small white mushrooms, finely sliced
2 shallots, finely chopped
4 tablespoons olive oil
1 clove garlic, crushed
1 tablespoon tomato purée
1 level teaspoon sugar
1 tablespoon chopped fresh marjoram
Salt, freshly ground black pepper

Heat the olive oil in a shallow saucepan or frying pan and gently cook the shallots until soft. Add the garlic. Turn up the heat and add the sliced mushrooms. Cook fairly fast for two minutes, then stir in the tomato purée, the sugar and the marjoram. Add the raw prawns or scampi (without any liquid) and simmer for a minute or two until they are tender. Allow to cool.

Dip the cherry tomatoes into boiling water for four or five seconds until the skins will come off easily. Peel them and cut them in half only if on the large side. Mix the mushroom and prawn mixture with the raw tomatoes, season well with salt and black pepper, and tip into a serving-dish. Scatter the chopped basil on top and chill before serving.

To serve:
5 or 6 fresh basil leaves, chopped

Serves 4–6

Celeriac remoulade

Make the sauce in advance but do not grate the celeriac into it more than two or three hours before serving. Will not freeze.

¾ lb (340 g) celeriac
½ pint (290 ml) mayonnaise
1 tablespoon pale French mustard
3 tablespoons single cream or soured cream
White pepper, salt
1 tablespoon lemon juice

Serves 6

Peel the celeriac thickly and put them into a basin of cold water to prevent discolouring (make sure they are submerged by floating a plate on top). Have ready the mayonnaise in a large mixing bowl, and mix into it the mustard, cream, seasoning and lemon juice.

Dry the celeriac and grate it straight into the mayonnaise, mixing it well as you do so. It is a mistake to grate the celeriac into water as this reduces the flavour and makes it mushy, and grating it onto a plate or into a dry bowl allows it to become badly discoloured. Mix well and add more salt and pepper if necessary.

Stuffed Starters

Things stuffed with other things always have a slightly festive air. Good melons or avocadoes need nothing doing to them at all, but sometimes the fruit is not quite perfect or for one reason or another something a little more elaborate is needed. The following recipes are suggestions for such occasions.

Stuffed cucumbers

As the juices from the cucumber are inclined to run out if this dish is made too long in advance, the cucumber blocks should not be filled until half an hour or so before serving. If they must be prepared well ahead they should first be lightly salted, left for half an hour to release their juices, then rinsed and patted dry before filling.

2 cucumbers
½ lb (225 g) good quality
  cream cheese
1 small carton soured
  cream
1 oz (30 g) walnuts,
  chopped
1 tablespoon chopped
  chives, dill or mint
Squeeze lemon juice
Salt, pepper

Using a potato peeler peel several long strips of skin from the whole cucumber, leaving alternate lengths unpeeled so that the cucumber has a stripey appearance. Cut the cucumber into pieces about 1 in (2½ cm) long. Lay them, cut side down, on the table top and scoop most of the flesh out of the middle of each block, using a melon baller or teaspoon.

Mix together all the remaining ingredients, adding sufficient lemon juice, salt and pepper to give a well-flavoured mixture. Put the scooped-out pieces of cucumber onto a serving dish and fill each one with a heaped teaspoon or two of the mixture.

Serves 4–6

Avocadoes filled with apple and crab

Almost every bistro in the country seems to serve avocado filled with prawns. We have nothing against such things, which can be delicious, but the crunchy texture of celery and apple, with the flavour of crab is, we think, even more delicious.

2 large ripe avocadoes
3 oz (85 g) white crab meat, either tinned or frozen
1 stick celery, finely chopped
2 tablespoons thick mayonnaise
1 tablespoon soured cream, or single cream
Juice and grated rind of ½ small lemon
1 dessert apple
1 dessertspoon chopped chives
A little oil
Salt, pepper

Serves 4

First make the filling. Sort through the white crab meat to extract any pieces of hard plastic-like cartilage. Flake the flesh into a bowl. Add the chopped celery and the mayonnaise, cream, the juice and grated rind of the lemon, and salt and pepper to taste. Add the chopped apple, stirring it in as you chop it so that it does not have time to discolour.

Split the avocado pears and remove the stones. Paint the avocado flesh with a little oil to prevent discoloration and fill neatly with the mixture. Scatter over the chives.

Melon stuffed with prawns and celery

Choose small Ogen melons. They are not as prohibitively expensive as the Charantais and come small enough for each person to have a whole melon (if it is very tiny) or half a larger one.

4 scooped-out half melons (or whole ones if very small)
1 stick celery, finely chopped
½ green pepper, finely chopped
¼ lb (110 g) peeled cooked prawns
2 tablespoons good mayonnaise (recipe p. 15)
2 tablespoons cream
1 dessertspoon tomato purée
1 dessertspoon lemon juice
Salt, freshly ground black pepper
Ground paprika

Serves 4

Mix together the mayonnaise, cream, tomato purée and lemon juice, and season with the salt and pepper. In a bowl mix together the chopped celery, chopped green pepper and prawns. Take half the mayonnaise mixture and stir it into this. Divide between the four scooped-out melons. Chill the melons well, and chill the remaining sauce.

Just before serving spoon over a little more sauce, which will look fresh and appetizing, and sprinkle lightly with paprika.

Tomatoes filled with ham and cottage cheese

The filling can be made well in advance for this dish, and the tomatoes peeled and scooped out. Indeed they will keep, even filled, in a refrigerator for six hours or so if covered with a piece of plastic film.

Herby French dressing spooned over the top of the tomatoes just before serving gives them a shiny look and, I think, improves the flavour, especially if a few fresh basil leaves are chopped and added to the dressing.

4 large tomatoes
   (preferably the wobbly
   Mediterranean kind)
2 thin slices ham, finely
   diced
¼ lb (110 g) cottage
   cheese
Salt, freshly ground black
   pepper

To serve:
Watercress

Bring a saucepan of water to the boil and drop the tomatoes into it for five seconds. Fish them out and skin them. Cut a thick slice from the rounded end of each tomato and keep these for the lids. Scoop most of the flesh from the tomatoes, taking care not to break the shells. Push the tomato pulp through a sieve to extract the seeds.

Mix the cottage cheese and ham together and add enough of the tomato juice to give a soft but not sloppy mixture. Season with salt and plenty of freshly ground black pepper and pile back into the tomato shells. Put back the lids at a jaunty angle and dish up with a sprig or two of watercress.

Serves 4

35

Patés and Dips

Avocado paté

There are dozens of avocado mixes, dips and spreads, and strict adherence to quantities given in recipes is not necessary. The essential is to beat the avocado pulp until absolutely smooth, and to season it well. The addition of cream cheese or mayonnaise makes it richer and blander. It will not freeze.

1 large ripe avocado pear, peeled and stoned
¼ lb (110 g) good quality cream cheese
Juice of ½ small lemon
1 clove garlic, crushed
Pinch dried ground coriander
3 tablespoons soured cream
Salt, pepper

Mix all the ingredients together except the soured cream, beating well to get an absolutely smooth paste. Put the mixture into a dish and spread the top entirely flat. Mix the soured cream with salt and pepper to taste and then spread it all over the top of the avocado. This will prevent the avocado mixture going an unappetizing grey.

Serves 4

Chicken liver paté

This is the simplest of chicken liver patés, and probably one of the best. It freezes well, but may be slightly crumbly on thawing.

6 oz (170 g) chicken livers
¼ lb (110 g) butter
1 medium onion, finely chopped
1 clove garlic, crushed
1 tablespoon brandy
Sprig of thyme

Serves 4

Trim any discoloured parts from the chicken livers. Melt half the butter in a large frying pan and in it gently cook the onions until they are soft and transparent. Add the garlic and the chicken livers, turn up the heat and fry fast to brown the livers. Turn them as they are frying, and when evenly browned all over lower the heat and cook gently until they feel firm to the touch (about seven or eight minutes). Add the brandy and thyme, and shake over the heat for half a minute more.

Push the contents of the frying pan, butter and all, through a sieve, or liquidize it in a blender. When the mixture is stone-cold beat in the remaining butter. Transfer to a small serving dish and chill before serving with hot bread or toast.

Taramasalata

Taramasalata is a Greek dip or soft spread made from smoked mullet or cod's roe. It is made much like mayonnaise: the oil must be beaten into the mixture very slowly to prevent curdling. It will keep for a week in a refrigerator but cannot be frozen.

½ lb (225 g) smoked cod's roe, skinned, or 1 small jar (about ¼ lb (110 g))
1 thick slice fresh white bread without the crusts
2 small cloves garlic, crushed
½ pint (290 ml) salad oil (or olive oil, or a mixture)
Freshly ground black pepper
Lemon juice
Salt if necessary

Soak the bread in water and squeeze it almost dry. Crumble it in a bowl. Add the cod's roe, making sure that you have removed any lumpy pieces of skin. Add the crushed garlic and a good few twists of black pepper. Beat this mixture into a thick paste. Now start to add the oil gradually, about a teaspoon at a time, beating vigorously between each addition. Keep adding the oil, and keep beating until you have a thick creamy, pale paste. Season with salt if necessary, and more black pepper. Add a good squeeze of lemon juice (up to half a lemon) and mix well. Keep covered until serving to prevent a skin forming.

Serves 6–8

Mock taramasalata

A good-tasting, though not classic, cod's roe paté can be made with cream cheese. Beat smoked cod's roe into good quality cream cheese and season well with salt and pepper, lemon juice and crushed garlic. It will freeze, but the texture is less smooth after thawing.

Smoked trout paté

Both the authors are against too much elaborate decoration, but this paté looks pretty and amusing, and does not take all day to decorate. The paté is served in our restaurant covered in thin slices of smoked salmon. But smoked salmon costing what it does, the dish is out of the financial reach of all but expense-account diners. This version is covered with finely sliced cucumber and is lighter and, we think, just as delicious. The paté mixture freezes well. Do not freeze with the cucumber in place.

3 small smoked trout, skinned and boned
½ pint (290 ml) double cream
1 level teaspoon creamed horseradish
Lemon juice
White pepper, salt

To serve:
½ cucumber

Serves 4

Peel the cucumber, slice it very finely and put the slices in a bowl. Add a dessertspoon of salt and just enough water to cover. Mix well and leave for at least half an hour. This salting is to extract some of the juices, which would otherwise run out when the cucumber comes in contact with the salted paté, and make the dish wet and unappetizing.

While the cucumber is soaking make the paté. Remove the bones and skin of the fish and put the flesh into a bowl. If you have a mixer with a slow whisk, all the better. Whisk the flesh and you will find that any remaining bones cling to the whisk head. Otherwise simply sort through the flesh carefully, extracting all the bones. Beat the cream until it is thick but not too stiff. Add the cream to the fish, and season with lemon juice, horseradish, salt and pepper. The mixture will probably be on the sloppy side. If it is, beat it with a whisk until it is the consistency of whipped cream. Put the mixture onto a flat plate and form it as best you can into the shape of a fish, or into a simple flattish mound.

Drain and rinse the cucumber and tip onto absorbent paper or onto a clean tea towel. Pat dry thoroughly. Lay the cucumber slices in overlapping rows all over the fish paté. If you have shaped the paté like a fish, the cucumber slices can be laid to represent scales, and the cucumber skin can be used to represent fins, tail and eye.

Squid and prawn salad

Thin strips of raw carrot make a good addition to this salad and give it a colourful appearance. Other seafood may be added too, such as mussels, scallops or lobster. The salad may be prepared five or six hours in advance.

1 lb (450 g) fresh squid, cleaned and, if possible, skinned
3 oz (85 g) peeled cooked prawns
Sprig fresh thyme (or pinch dried thyme)
1 bay leaf
3 oz (85 g) white button mushrooms
1 medium-sized mild onion
½ green pepper
2 or 3 sprigs parsley

For the dressing:
3 tablespoons salad oil
1 dessertspoon mild wine vinegar
Lemon juice
Salt, freshly ground black pepper
1 clove garlic, crushed
1 tablespoon chopped fresh parsley
1 teaspoon chopped fresh thyme

Cut the squid into thin strips and put it in a saucepan. Cover with cold water and add the parsley stalks, half the onion, the sprig of thyme and the bay leaf. Give a twist or two with the peppermill, then bring gently to simmering point. Simmer until the squid is tender (between twenty and thirty-five minutes). Leave to cool in the water.

Slice the mushrooms and put them in a bowl. Chop the rest of the onion finely and add to the mushrooms. Slice the green pepper as finely as you can, discarding stalk, seeds and pith. Put in the bowl with the squid and prawns.

To make the dressing combine the oil, vinegar, lemon juice, crushed garlic, chopped parsley, and season well with salt and pepper. Whisk until well emulsified, then pour over the salad mixture. Mix well so that all the ingredients are coated with dressing. Chill for two or three hours before serving. Sprinkle with chopped fresh thyme if you have it. Dried thyme won't do.

Serves 4–6

Whole boned duck

This recipe takes time, and needs to be started at least twenty-four hours in advance, but the result does justify the effort.

1 boned duck
1½ lb (675 g) pork belly, boneless and skinless
½ lb (225 g) duck and/or chicken livers, cleaned
½ teaspoon mixed spice
1 egg
2 oz (55 g) plain flour
Good pinch rubbed thyme
Pepper, salt
¼ lb (110 g) onions, sliced
Finely grated rind of 1 orange
1 liqueur glass brandy

Serves 6–8

If the duck cannot be bought ready-boned, this is how to tackle it. The main point to remember is to keep the boning knife as close to the bone as possible, scraping and easing the flesh away carefully. A short flexible knife is essential. Turn the bird breast side down and cut through the skin, along the backbone, from the parson's nose to the neck. Work the skin and flesh away from the bones, peeling back the flesh as you go, gradually exposing the rib cage. When you get to the legs and wings, cut through the tendons close against the carcass at the joints. This will mean that the wings and legs stay attached to the skin, not to the carcass. Continue working round the bird, taking special care when boning the breast where the skin and bone are very close. If the wings and legs are to be boned too, chop off the wing pinions and the knuckle-end of the drumsticks. Working from the thicker end of the joints ease the bones out, scraping the flesh from them carefully. It may be necessary to work from the drumstick or the wing tip ends as well, but most of the work should be done from the body side. Cut off any excess fat, especially from near the parson's nose.

When all the bones are out scrape off any flesh still adhering to them and keep it to add to the stuffing.

The meat should be marinated overnight. To do this lay the duck in a deep container, sprinkling it with mixed spice, salt and pepper, the thyme, sliced onions, orange rind and juice. Pour over the brandy and season well. Dice the pork belly into 1 in (2½ cm) cubes, and lay on top of the duck, pressing down well. Keep cool.

Next day, mince all the pork belly, the onions and the duck or chicken livers. Add the flour, mix well, then add the egg and any juices from the overnight marinade.

Open the duck out on a board, skin side down. Smear well with some of the stuffing mix (this helps to prevent paté and duck flesh separating when sliced). Spoon the paté down the centre of the duck, roll up and press to eliminate trapped air bubbles (they leave unsightly, greyish holes after cooking). Bring the two edges of skin together and sew up tightly, from one end to the other, using fine string.

To cook the stuffed duck, place it in a roasting tin, in a pre-heated oven (180°C/350°F/ Gas Mark 4) for two hours of slow cooking. Turn once to ensure an even colour. Cover with aluminium foil if in danger of over-browning. The paté is cooked when it feels firm to the touch, and when the juices from the thickest part run out clear, not pink, when the paté is pierced. Allow to cool, then refrigerate before slicing.

Cold tarragon chicken

This is a marvellous variation on the perennial summer cold chicken. It is all the better for being prepared a day in advance, and even when the sauce is in place it can be wrapped loosely with a piece of plastic wrap and kept in a cool place for three or four hours before serving. Do not freeze it.

3 lb (1.35 kg) roasting chicken, untrussed
1 teaspoon bouillon mix or a stock cube
1 carton sour cream
1 carton yogurt
¼ pint (150 ml) good mayonnaise
3 or 4 sprigs fresh tarragon, chopped
Salt, pepper

Serves 4–5

First boil the chicken. Put it with all its giblets (except the liver) and the neck into a saucepan into which it fits snugly. Cover with water and add the stock cube or bouillon mix. Put on a lid and simmer gently until the chicken is tender and the drumsticks will wobble loosely when moved. Do not take the chicken out of the stock to cool it but stand the whole saucepan in a large bowl of cold water, so contriving things that the cold tap drips into the water and keeps it cool. This way the chicken will not dry out as it cools but can still be cooled rapidly.

Mix together the mayonnaise, sour cream, yogurt and tarragon and flavour with salt and pepper as necessary. You should have a very thick mixture.

When the chicken is completely cold lift it out and skin it. Cut the joints into neat pieces (or if preferred remove all the flesh from the chicken: this is obviously more suitable if the chicken is to be eaten standing up). Arrange the chicken pieces on a dish. Mix sufficient of the chicken stock with the creamy mayonnaise sauce to give a sauce of coating consistency. It should run reluctantly off the spoon and stay covering the chicken nicely. Put the extra sauce into a bowl or sauceboat.

41

Salmon, seafood and turbot in tarragon aspic, with tomato cream

This jellied fish dish is exceptionally pretty, the pink and white of fish caught in the clear tarragon-flavoured aspic. It can be sliced in advance, or served whole, either turned out or from a terrine or dish. The sauce is light and, though luxurious, the dish is not rich or calorie-laden. Best eaten very fresh. It will not freeze.

½ lb (225 g) fresh salmon, diced into ½ in (1 cm) cubes
½ lb (225 g) fresh turbot, diced into ½ in (1 cm) cubes
6 oz (170 g) raw scampi (may be frozen)
½ pint (290 ml) white wine
5 oz (140 g) fish stock or water
1 oz (30 g) chopped tarragon
2 oz (55 g) chopped shallots
¼ oz (8 g) powdered gelatine
2 tablespoons water
Salt, pepper

For the sauce:
1 small pot plain yogurt
Small bunch chives, chopped
2 tomatoes, peeled and seeded
1 tablespoon tomato ketchup

Serves 5–6

Soak the gelatine in two tablespoons cold water. Pour the wine and the water (or fish stock) into a pan. Add the fish and scampi. Add salt and pepper and bring to simmering point. Poach very gently for three minutes. With a perforated spoon lift the fish carefully into a bowl.

Pass the stock through a sieve fitted with a coffee filter paper or fine muslin. Return it to the pan, add the shallots, chopped tarragon and the softened gelatine. Check the seasoning and simmer for a few more minutes until the gelatine is dissolved. Place the cooked fish in a mould. Pour over all the stock. Shake gently to get the shallots and tarragon to mix evenly through the fish. Allow to cool, then refrigerate until set. If liked the fish mould can be dipped in hot water and turned out like a jelly.

To make the sauce, liquidize or sieve the peeled tomatoes. Add the yogurt, ketchup, a few twists of the peppermill and the chives. Mix and pour into a sauceboat. Serve the sauce separately.

German salad

The dressing can be made for this salad well in advance and the ingredients prepared. Do not mix them together more than an hour or so before serving.

2 frankfurters
½ lb (225 g) German smoked beer sausage in a piece
4 ripe tomatoes
4 small cooked potatoes, peeled
¼ lb (110 g) Dutch white cabbage, finely shredded

For the dressing :
4 tablespoons salad oil
1 tablespoon red wine vinegar
½ teaspoon sugar
Pinch salt
1 large clove garlic, crushed
1 level tablespoon English or German mustard
Pinch coarsely ground nutmeg
1 tablespoon chopped chives
1 tablespoon chopped parsley

Slice the frankfurters in thick diagonal slices. Skin the beer sausage and cut it into even dice. Dip the tomatoes in boiling water for five seconds, then slip off their skins, and cut in quarters. Cut the cooked potato into cubes. Put the frankfurters, sausage, cabbage, tomatoes and potatoes into a large bowl.

For the dressing put all the ingredients together in a screw-top jar. Shake well until emulsified, or whisk with a fork. Pour over the salad ingredients, and using your hands (for speed and efficiency) mix well. Tip the salad into a clean serving-dish and chill well.

Serves 4 generously

43

Mackerel fillets Provençale

This dish can be made the day before it is to be eaten. Do not be tempted to freeze it, however – this spoils the texture of the fish.

¾ lb (340 g) mackerel
    fillets
2 oz (55 g) onion,
    chopped
1 large clove garlic,
    crushed
1 tablespoon tomato
    purée
¼ pint (150 ml) water
2 tablespoons wine
    vinegar
3 fresh tomatoes, peeled
    and chopped
1 bouquet garni: bay leaf,
    sprig thyme, stick
    celery and a few
    parsley stalks tied
    together with string
Salt, freshly ground black
    pepper

Sprinkle the chopped onion into a shallow pan or tray. Wash each fish fillet and cut into four or five pieces. Lay them in the tray. Mix the garlic, tomato purée, the water, vinegar, salt and pepper together and pour over the mackerel pieces. Sprinkle the chopped tomatoes on top, and add the bouquet garni and a sprinkling of pepper and salt.

Cook in a pre-heated oven, 220°C/425°F/ Gas Mark 7, for about twenty minutes or until the fish feels firm. Remove from the oven and allow to cool overnight. Remove the bouquet garni and re-dish the fish and its sauce. Add salt if necessary.

Serves 4

Green mayonnaise eggs

This sort of egg starter is particularly good served with brown bread and butter sprinkled with chopped walnuts. Press the walnuts into the butter to make sure they stay in place.

6 hard-boiled eggs
⅓ pint (190 ml)
    mayonnaise
3 tablespoons cream
1 small bunch watercress
2 or 3 spinach leaves
Squeeze lemon juice
Salt, freshly ground black
    pepper

Remove the hard stalks from the watercress and spinach leaves and wash the leaves well. Put them, still wet, into a saucepan. Do not add any more water but put on a lid. Holding the handle of the pan in one hand and the lid on with the other, shake the pan over high heat, tossing the contents for about a minute until the leaves are soft and reduced in bulk but still bright green. Tip out and allow to cool.

Put the mayonnaise into a liquidizer and add the cooked leaves. Blend until smooth and uniformly green. Season with salt, pepper and lemon juice to taste and stir in the cream.

Split the eggs lengthwise and lay them, flat side down, on a serving dish. Spoon over the green mayonnaise.

Serves 4

Hot Starters, Savouries & Supper Dishes

Soups

Crab bisque

The cost of crab being what it is, few people would buy a crab to make a soup. But if you have the shell and legs left over from a crab dish, or can buy small or cracked crabs cheaply, make this bisque. It is wonderful.

The shell(s) and other remains of one large or several small crabs
2 oz (55 g) tomato purée
5 tablespoons dry white wine
5 tablespoons brandy
1 small bunch tarragon or (if unavailable) parsley
2 cloves garlic
1 bouquet garni: bay leaf, sprig thyme, a few parsley stalks tied together with string
3 oz (85 g) onions, finely chopped
3 oz (85 g) carrots, finely chopped
3 oz (85 g) celery, finely chopped
¼ pint (150 ml) double cream
3 oz (85 g) butter
1¾ pints (1 litre) water
1½ oz (45 g) flour
Salt, pepper
Pinch chilli powder
Crisply fried bread croûtons

Crush all the bones and shells of the crab by pounding them in a mortar or in a tough bowl with one end of the rolling pin.

Heat 1 oz (30 g) of the butter and gently fry all the chopped vegetables, the garlic, the tarragon and the bouquet garni until the onions are soft. Add the tomato purée and chilli powder, stir, then add all the crushed bones and the wine and brandy. Pour in the water and simmer for forty minutes.

Melt the remaining butter in the rinsed-out saucepan and stir in the flour. Draw the pan off the heat and blend in the strained liquid. Stir until boiling. Simmer for two minutes, then check the seasoning. Add cream just before serving, with croûtons handed separately.

Serves 4–5

47

Lentil and bacon soup

This soup will keep refrigerated for up to a week, and the flavour remains excellent. It freezes well too. Thaw before bringing to simmering point. Do not boil.

3 oz (85 g) red lentils
2 rashers bacon
2 oz (55 g) chopped onions
¼ lb (110 g) sliced raw potato
Salt, pepper
1½ pints (860 ml) stock (or water and a bouillon cube)
Teaspoon butter if needed

Cut the fat and rind from the bacon rashers, and fry them to extract their fat. Remove them and replace with the chopped onion. Fry slowly until soft, adding a little butter if needed.

Finely dice the lean part of the bacon, add it to the pan and fry slowly. Now add the lentils, the slices of potato and the stock. Season with pepper and salt and simmer until all the ingredients are cooked. Press through a vegetable mill or blender. Check the seasoning.

Serve with the crisp fried bread croûtons handed separately.

To serve:
Fried bread dice (croûtons)

Serves 4

Artichoke and spinach soup

This soup freezes excellently. If it is to be made more than six or seven hours in advance I would rather freeze it than leave it in an ordinary refrigerator. Vegetable soups left in the refrigerator lose their freshness rapidly.

1 oz (30 g) butter
½ medium onion, finely chopped
½ lb (225 g) Jerusalem artichokes, peeled
1¼ pints (720 ml) good chicken stock
6 oz (170 g) young spinach leaves
Salt, freshly ground white pepper
Grated nutmeg
¾ pint (425 ml) milk
3 tablespoons cream

Wash the spinach and remove the stalks. Melt the butter in a large saucepan and cook the chopped onion until it is soft and transparent looking. Slice the artichokes finely and add them to the pan. Put on a lid and allow to 'sweat' for ten minutes or so, occasionally giving the pan a good shake. Add the chicken stock and bring to the boil. Season to taste with salt, pepper and nutmeg. Simmer until the artichokes are cooked.

Add the washed spinach to the soup and whizz it in a liquidizer. In the absence of a liquidizer the spinach can be briefly cooked in the stock before the whole soup is put through a vegetable mill or sieve. Add the milk, reheat the soup and stir in the cream. The soup is good hot or cold.

Serves 5–6

Artichoke and leek soup

Freeze the soup if you are not going to serve it on the day it is cooked. Take care when thawing and reheating not to allow it to boil or it may curdle.

½ lb (225 g) Jerusalem artichokes
1 medium sized potato
1 large or 3 small leeks
2 oz (55 g) butter
1 small clove garlic, crushed
2 pints (1.15 l) chicken stock
Salt, pepper
Grated nutmeg
Lemon juice
1 tablespoon white port (optional)
2 tablespoons cream

Peel the potato and artichokes and chop them up fairly finely. Cut off and discard most of the green part of the leek and make sure that you have washed out all the soil and grit from the white part. Chop this roughly and put it with the artichokes and the potato into a large saucepan. Add the butter and stir until melted. Add the crushed garlic and put on a well-fitting lid.

Leave to cook gently, undisturbed, for five minutes and then give the pan a good shake. Continue, shaking occasionally for fifteen minutes or so or until the leeks look cooked and soft and the potato and artichokes are beginning to soften. Add the chicken stock and season with salt, pepper, lemon juice and nutmeg. Bring to the boil and simmer for thirty minutes or until the vegetables are very tender. Push the soup through a vegetable mill or sieve, or blend until smooth in a liquidizer.

Heat carefully without boiling, adding the white port and cream just before serving.

Serves 4

Leith's Stilton soup

This soup can be made several days in advance, and as long as it is not boiled when reheating it will not curdle. It freezes fairly well but it is difficult to reconstitute without curdling.

1 medium-sized onion or 4 shallots
2 sticks celery
2 tablespoons butter
1½ tablespoons flour
1¾ pints (1 litre) good chicken or veal stock
¼ cup dry white wine
½ pint (290 ml) milk
½ lb (225 g) crumbled Stilton cheese
3 tablespoons thick cream
Salt, pepper

Finely chop the onion and the celery and soften in the butter over gentle heat. Add the flour, and stir for a minute or two. Take the saucepan off the heat, and stir in the white wine and the stock. Bring to the boil, stirring. Simmer for three-quarters of an hour, or until the wine has lost its harsh alcoholic flavour. Add the milk, cream and the cheese. Allow the cheese to melt without boiling. Season with salt and pepper. For a smooth velvety texture liquidize the soup, or push it through a sieve. Serve hot with croûtons or cheese straws, or well chilled.

To serve:
Croûtons or cheese straws

Serves 4

Mrs Beeton's almond soup

This is something of a liberty since we have substituted chicken stock for beef stock, reduced the quantities enormously, and used egg yolk raw rather than hard-boiled and rubbed through a sieve. But the basic recipe comes from Mrs Beeton and we hope and believe she would approve our version. The soup will keep successfully for four or five days in an ordinary refrigerator, or it can be frozen successfully for up to a month or so. Longer freezing is not advisable because the almonds can develop a slightly rancid flavour. If the soup is to be frozen it should not contain the egg and cream, which can be added after reheating.

2 pints (1.15 l) good
   chicken stock
1 small onion, chopped
½ oz (15 g) butter
½ oz (15 g) flour
¼ lb (110 g) sweet
   almonds, blanched
Pinch cloves
Small blade mace (or
   pinch ground mace)
Salt, pepper
2 large egg yolks
5 tablespoons double
   cream

Melt the butter and gently cook the onion until soft and transparent looking. Stir in the flour and then the chicken stock. Add the mace and the cloves and stir until the stock has boiled. Simmer for ten minutes, then strain into a jug.

Put the almonds into a coffee grinder or liquidizer and grind them, taking care not to overdo it – they must not become oily. Whisk the almonds with a tablespoon or so of cream in a large bowl. Blend a spoon or two of the strained stock into the almond mixture and continue slowly adding soup until all is incorporated, and the soup is quite smooth. Taste and add salt or pepper if necessary.

Just before serving reheat the soup slowly while mixing together the egg yolks and the rest of the cream in a cup. Pour a ladleful or so of soup onto the egg yolk mixture and stir well. Tip this back into the soup and stir. Reheat, taking great care that the soup does not get near boiling point.

Serves 4–5

Egg Dishes

Poached eggs with bacon and burgundy sauce

These eggs make a banquet out of a supper dish. The sauce takes time and care but can be made well in advance. The eggs may even be poached in advance, leaving only the final warming up in the sauce and the frying of the bread for the last minute. It is most important to use really fresh eggs, and they should be straight from the fridge to prevent the white spreading in the poaching water.

4 very fresh eggs
1 pint (570 ml) water
5 tablespoons vinegar
Crisply fried cubes of
   bread

For the sauce:
2 oz (55g) streaky bacon,
   chopped
2 shallots, finely chopped
8 fluid oz (235 ml) red
   wine
8 fluid oz (235 ml) beef
   stock
Pinch rubbed thyme
Salt, pepper
1 oz (30 g) butter
1 tablespoon flour

To make the sauce boil the wine until reduced by half. Melt the butter in a small stewpan. Gently fry the bacon in it, then add the chopped shallots and cook until just turning colour. Stir in the flour. Remove from the heat, add the wine and stock and stir vigorously with a whisk. Return to the heat and stir until boiling. Simmer (for at least fifteen minutes) until the right syrupy consistency is achieved. Add the pepper and thyme, and salt only if the bacon is not sufficiently salted.

Now poach the eggs. Bring a pint of unsalted water and the vinegar near to boiling point in a fairly shallow pan (salt in the water spells disaster – the whites spread all over the water, leaving the yolks sadly on their own). One by one break the eggs into the water and keep near to boiling for three minutes. Remove the eggs with a perforated spoon and slip them into a dish full of cold water to prevent them cooking further. Dry the eggs on a piece of absorbent cloth or paper. When ready to serve re-warm the eggs gently in the sauce, remembering they must stay soft inside. Place on individual warmed serving plates and scatter the fried cubes of bread on top. Serve immediately.

Serves 4

51

Baked egg with onion cream sauce

Another simple egg dish, with little work to do at the last minute provided the onion sauce is prepared in advance.

1 medium, strongly
  flavoured onion, finely
  chopped
1½ oz (45 g) butter
½ oz (15 g) flour
7 fluid oz (200 ml) milk
3 tablespoons cream
Salt, white pepper
4 eggs

Serves 4

Melt the butter in a saucepan and add the finely chopped onion. Cook over a gentle heat until the onion is soft and transparent. Stir in the flour and cook for thirty seconds or so. Draw the pan off the heat and add the milk. Mix, then return to the heat and stir steadily until boiling. Season well with salt and pepper. Simmer for thirty seconds, add the cream and remove from the heat.

Put a spoonful of this sauce into the bottom of four ramekin dishes. Break an egg into each ramekin, and spoon the rest of the sauce over the top of the eggs. Stand the ramekin dishes in a deep frying pan or shallow sauté dish. Pour boiling water into the pan to come at least halfway up the sides of the ramekins. Cover with a lid or foil and set over a moderate heat. The water should simmer gently for six minutes, by which time the egg whites should be set but the yolks still runny. Lift out the ramekins, dry them underneath, and serve immediately.

Tarragon eggs

These eggs must be cooked at the last minute, but they can be ready-prepared in their buttered dishes and sitting in their sauté pan. This means that only the hot water needs to be added and the eggs set to cook.

4 eggs, the fresher the
  better
4 tablespoons double
  cream
8 leaves fresh tarragon
Salt, pepper
A little butter

Serves 4

Use the butter to grease four ramekin dishes. Break an egg into each. Put two tarragon leaves on top of each egg and spoon over a tablespoon of cream. Season with salt and pepper.

Stand the ramekin dishes in a fairly deep frying pan or sauté pan. Pour boiling water into the pan so that it comes at least half way up the ramekin dishes. Cover with a lid or piece of foil. Set the pan over a medium heat so that the water is kept simmering. After six minutes the whites of the egg should be set, but the yolks still runny. Lift out the ramekins, dry them underneath, and serve at once.

Baked egg with sorrel

The eggs must of course be cooked at the last minute, but if everything is got ready in advance this is little trouble.

4 eggs
2 or 3 young sorrel leaves
1 shallot, finely chopped
1 oz (30 g) butter
4 tablespoons cream
Salt, pepper

Serves 4

Melt the butter in a frying pan and add the finely chopped shallot. Cook very slowly until the shallot looks transparent. Shred the sorrel leaves finely and add them, with salt and pepper.

Divide this mixture, including the butter, between four ramekin dishes, making sure that the sides of the ramekins are well greased. Break an egg into each dish and add a tablespoon of cream to each one. Stand the ramekin dishes in a deep frying pan or shallow sauté dish. Pour boiling water into the pan to come at least halfway up the sides of the ramekins.

Cover with a lid or foil and set over a moderate heat. The water should simmer gently for six minutes, by which time the egg whites should be set but the yolks still runny. Lift out the ramekins, dry them underneath, and serve immediately.

Stuffed eggs with cheese and tomatoes

This dish can be entirely prepared in advance, leaving only the last-minute reheating and browning of the top until just before serving. Do not be tempted to freeze; hard-boiled egg whites become leathery and unpalatable if frozen.

4 hard-boiled eggs
2½ oz (70g) butter
1 medium onion, chopped
1 tablespoon chopped fresh basil
1 clove garlic, crushed
1½ oz (45 g) Gruyère cheese
1 small Mozzarella cheese
1 tablespoon stale white breadcrumbs
½ lb (225 g) tomatoes
½ pint (290 ml) milk
¾ oz (20 g) flour
Salt, white pepper

Serves 4

Melt 1 oz (30 g) of the butter in a saucepan and slowly cook the onion until soft and transparent. Add the crushed garlic and stir in the flour. Cook for thirty seconds, then remove from the heat and pour in the milk. Stir well, return to the heat and bring to the boil, stirring all the time. Season fairly heavily with white pepper and lightly with salt.

Cut the Gruyère into small chunks and stir it into the sauce. Dip the tomatoes in boiling water for five seconds. Peel them and slice them coarsely. Melt 1 oz (30 g) of the butter in a frying pan and quickly fry the tomato slices until half cooked. Tip them, and the juices from the pan, into the bottom of a pie-dish.

Cut the hard-boiled eggs in half lengthways and scoop out the yolks. Add the remaining ½ oz (15 g) butter to the yolks and mash to a smooth paste. Work in the tablespoon of chopped basil and then stuff this mixture back into the egg white halves. Slice the Mozzarella cheese and lay the slices on top of the tomatoes. Then put the stuffed eggs on top of the Mozzarella, and pour the cheese sauce all over the top. Sprinkle with the breadcrumbs. Bake in a hot oven to brown the top, and reheat the dish (about ten minutes).

Hidden eggs

In appearance this dish is no more glamorous than a Scotch egg bought in a pub. But if made correctly, the yolk, when the egg is cut, will still be runny, giving a rich and delicious sauce to the mushroom and spinach coating. It is a good combination of crisp coating and rich soft middle. It can be prepared in advance up to the egg and breadcrumb stage, leaving only the final deep frying for the last minute.

4 eggs
2 shallots, very finely chopped
½ lb (225 g) mushrooms, finely chopped
½ lb (225 g) spinach
2 oz (55 g) butter
2 oz (55 g) flour
About ¼ pint (150 ml) stock
Salt, freshly ground black pepper
A little extra flour for rolling
1 beaten egg
Dry white breadcrumbs
Oil for deep frying

Serves 4

With a needle prick a tiny hole in the rounded end of each egg. Bring a small saucepan of water to the boil, gently lower in the eggs and cook for five minutes if they are large, four if on the small side. Immediately put the saucepan under the cold water tap and let the water run until the eggs are completely cold. Peel them very carefully, and pat them dry with a clean tea towel.

To make the spinach and mushroom coating wash the spinach, removing any tough stalks, and dunk it for a minute in boiling water. Lift it out with a perforated spoon, while it is still bright green, and squeeze out all the moisture, either between two plates or in a tea towel, or (when it is cold enough to handle) in your hands.

Melt the butter in a small saucepan, add the finely chopped shallot and cook slowly until transparent and soft. Add the chopped mushrooms and stir over the heat for a minute or so or until the mushrooms are soft. Stir in the flour, cook for thirty seconds and then stir in most of the stock. Stir steadily over the heat until you have a thick paste. Allow it to bubble briefly, adding salt and pepper to taste. Put the thick sauce, and the spinach leaves into a liquidizer and blend to a fine paste. In the absence of a liquidizer push everything through a sieve, or mash it in a pestle and mortar. Allow the paste to get stone-cold.

Divide the mixture into four and flatten it with your hands (if the hands are floured lightly the mixture will stick to them less). Use each piece to envelop one egg completely. This is a little tricky to do, but not as difficult as it sounds. Make sure the joins are well pressed together. Chill well, which will harden the coating, making it easier to handle.

Roll the coated eggs first in seasoned flour, then in beaten egg, and finally in the dry white breadcrumbs. Keep refrigerated until needed. Ten minutes before serving, heat the oil in the deep fryer until it is hot enough to make a breadcrumb sizzle vigorously. Fry the eggs, all together, until the crumbs are a good golden brown. This should not take longer than two minutes. Drain them well on absorbent paper, and serve at once.

Arnold Bennett eggs

I'm told that this recipe should not contain tomato. In fact I believe classically 'Arnold Bennett' should apply only to a smoked haddock omelette, not a baked egg at all. But this is how we have always done them and they are delicious. They must be cooked at the last minute. Provided the eggs are in their buttered dishes with the other ingredients and the boiling water and frying pan at the ready they are easy to cook in spite of last-minute work.

¼ lb (110 g) smoked
   haddock fillet
2 or 3 tablespoons milk
4 tablespoons double
   cream
1 large tomato
4 eggs
A little butter
Salt, pepper

Serves 4

First poach the haddock. Put it into a small frying pan, pour on the milk and cover with a lid or piece of foil. Set over gentle heat for three or four minutes until the flesh no longer looks glassy. Butter four ramekin dishes and divide the haddock, fairly finely flaked, between them.

Dip the tomato into boiling water for five seconds (or hold it over the gas flame on the end of a fork) to loosen the skin. Peel, quarter and de-seed it. Cut the quarters into small pieces and divide between the ramekins. Break an egg into each ramekin and spoon over a tablespoon of cream. Season sparingly with salt and fairly well with pepper.

Stand the ramekin dishes in a deep frying pan or shallow sauté pan and pour enough boiling water into the pan to come at least halfway up the sides of the dishes. Cover the pan with a lid or piece of foil and set over a moderate heat so that the water simmers. After six minutes the yolks of the egg should still be runny, but the whites nicely set.

Savouries

Soft herring roes on toast

If you can get them fresh, soft roes are a real treat. (Make sure you are buying soft, not hard, roes. Hard roes are a disaster.) If not the tinned ones make a good substitute.

If they are fresh and raw fry them, briefly, in hot butter with a little lemon juice and slip them onto buttered toast.

Tinned roes are already cooked of course and only need reheating in a little butter.

Sprinkle with lemon juice and serve at once.

Mushrooms and anchovies on toast

This is such a simple dish it seems a bit cheeky to include it in a sophisticated cook book. But it is so delicious we cannot resist it, and besides it makes a useful lunch or supper dish, if not served as a savoury after dinner.

4 rounds white bread
About 1 oz (30 g) butter
½ lb (225 g) small white Paris mushrooms
1 tin anchovies
Squeeze lemon juice
½ clove garlic, crushed

To serve:
Chopped parsley

Serves 4

Toast the bread and cut it into neat rounds, squares or octagonal shapes. Crush the garlic and mix it with about 1 oz (30 g) of butter. Use this mixture to butter the four pieces of shaped toast. Keep warm. Take the anchovies from their tin, tipping the oil into a frying pan. Split the anchovies lengthwise to give thin strings of anchovy fillet. Fry the mushrooms (with the stalks trimmed back) in the oil from the anchovy tin. Fry them fairly fast so that they brown: they should cook in about four minutes.

When cooked arrange them carefully, rounded side up, on the pieces of toast. Use the thin anchovy fillet strips to lattice the top of the mushrooms on toast and squeeze a very little lemon juice over each portion. Just before serving sprinkle with chopped parsley.

Devilled sardines on toast

These are best made with fresh or frozen sardines but the tinned ones, though different, are good too.

Sardines
Toast
Butter
Anchovy essence
English mustard
Lemon juice
Chopped parsley
Black pepper

Spread slices of toast with a strongly flavoured butter made by beating anchovy essence, English mustard and lemon juice into the softened butter. Grill the sardines in the usual way if they are raw; if they are tinned, simply remove them from the tin, and heat in a frying pan. If using fresh fish, remove the heads and bones once they are cooked. Put the pieces of sardine, or the whole tinned sardines, on the toast and grind plenty of black pepper over them. Sprinkle with a little lemon juice and scatter chopped parsley over them before serving.

L'anchoïade aux tomates

A substantial salty snack – good for lunch or supper or as a fairly hefty starter. The anchovy mixture keeps well in the refrigerator, and will freeze if necessary. Frying the bread and assembling the anchoïade must be done à la minute.

1 small tin anchovy fillets in olive oil
4 large tomatoes, peeled
Pinch rubbed dry thyme or 1 teaspoon chopped fresh thyme
2 oz (55 g) chopped onions
Freshly ground pepper
1 tablespoon olive oil
2 small cloves garlic, crushed
4 small slices bread without crusts
Butter for frying

Slice one tomato into four thickish slices. Chop the rest. Heat the olive oil in a frying pan and fry the chopped onions until golden, then add the chopped tomatoes, the thyme, the crushed garlic and season with salt and pepper. Simmer until most of the tomato liquid has evaporated, and you have a thick mixture. Check the seasoning.

Fry the bread on both sides in butter until brown and crisp. Place the slices in a serving dish. Cover them with the cooked tomato. Put a slice of tomato on each, then arrange the anchovy fillets on top to form a lattice. If you like garlic crush another clove in a small cup and mix with the oil from the anchovy tin. Sprinkle the oil (with or without the extra garlic) on top of the anchoïade.

Place the dish under the grill until the top is gently bubbling. Sprinkle with chopped parsley and serve.

To serve:
1 tablespoon chopped parsley

Serves 4

Mussels in parsley and garlic butter

The mussels may be boiled four or five hours before serving but should be kept in a cool place until they are baked. The parsley and garlic butter can be spread over them so that the only last-minute work will be the actual baking.

2 pints (1.15 l) or 2 lb (900 g) live mussels
1 onion, chopped
Cupful water

For the butter:
1 large clove garlic, crushed
1 or 2 shallots, very finely chopped
3 tablespoons finely chopped parsley
¼ lb (110 g) butter
Salt, black pepper

For the topping:
1 tablespoon grated Parmesan cheese
1 tablespoon dried, browned breadcrumbs

Serves 4–6

Scrub the mussels well in the sink, pulling of the beards and discarding any that will not close firmly when you tap them on the sink edge. Put the mussels into a large saucepan and scatter over the chopped onion. Add the cup of water and put on the lid. Hold, shaking occasionally, over a fairly brisk heat until all the mussels have opened – three or four minutes. Allow to cool, leaving the saucepan lid half on to prevent them drying out. While they are cooling make the butter.

Work together the crushed garlic, the chopped shallot, the chopped parsley and the butter until you have a smooth soft paste. Add a little salt and plenty of black pepper.

Once the mussels are cool enough to handle break each one apart and throw away the top shell. Remove the 'rubber band' from around each mussel and discard it. Spread the garlic butter all over each mussel, then put them, still in their bottom shells, onto oven-proof dinner plates or dishes (serving is a lot easier if individual plates are baked in the oven). Mix the breadcrumbs and cheese together and use to sprinkle evenly all over the top of the mussels. Half an hour before dinner heat the oven to 200°C/400°F/Gas Mark 6. Ten minutes before serving put the mussels into the oven, near the top, to brown.

Mackerel with saffron rice pescador

Both rice and mackerel mixture can be cooked a day in advance and kept in larder or refrigerator. Freezing is a mistake, however, as the mackerel texture is lost on thawing.

For the yellow pilau rice:
6 oz (170 g) (1 tea cup) Patna rice (long grain)
12 fluid oz (345 ml) water
1 tablespoon olive oil
1 oz (30 g) onion, chopped
Pinch ground saffron or saffron shreds
½ teaspoon turmeric powder
1 bay leaf
1 clove
Salt

For the mackerel:
¾ lb (340 g) mackerel fillet cut into 2-in (5 cm) pieces
1 tablespoon olive oil
2 oz (55 g) onion, chopped
2 garlic cloves, crushed
1 oz (30 g) celery, chopped
2 large tomatoes, peeled and chopped
1 tablespoon tomato purée
Pinch cayenne pepper
Salt, pepper
6 fluid oz (175 ml) water

Serves 4

First make the pilau. Bring the water to the boil. At the same time warm the oil in a small stewpan and in it gently fry the chopped onion until just golden, then add the rice, a sprinkling of salt, the saffron, turmeric, clove and bay leaf. Stir well and pour in the boiling water. Cover with a lid and simmer slowly until all the water has evaporated (about twenty-five minutes). Taste, and if the rice is still hard in the middle of the grain add a little water and keep cooking under the lid a few minutes longer.

To cook the mackerel, heat the olive oil in a frying pan, gently fry the chopped onion until soft, then the crushed garlic for half a minute. Add the chopped celery and tomatoes, the tomato purée, all the seasonings and the water. Stir, and check the seasoning. Place the pieces of fish side by side in the pan. If they are not covered by the sauce, spoon some over them. Cover with a lid and simmer for ten minutes.

Arrange the hot yellow rice round the edge of a serving-dish. Put the fish in the middle and spoon over a little sauce. Serve the remaining sauce separately.

Dublin Bay prawn pancakes

Real Dublin Bay prawns are almost impossible to get these days. The essential is that the prawn, crayfish tail, or langoustine should be raw before use. Cooked frozen prawns are too flavourless to give a good result. The stuffed pancakes may be frozen. They should be thawed before reheating and browning the top.

For the filling :
½ lb (225 g) raw peeled
   Dublin Bay prawns,
   scampi, or crayfish tails
4 scallops
½ bay leaf
A few peppercorns
Slice or two onion
Small bunch parsley
Salt
¾ oz (20 g) butter
¾ oz (20 g) flour
4 fluid oz (110 ml) milk

8 large thin French
   pancakes (recipe p. 73)

Beaten egg

Oil for deep frying

To serve :
Spicy tomato sauce
   (optional) (recipe p. 14)
Grated cheese (optional)

Serves 4

If the scampi are frozen allow them to thaw slowly overnight in the fridge. Put them, and any juice they have, or the raw Dublin Bay prawns or crayfish tails and the four raw scallops into a saucepan and add the bay leaf, peppercorns, slice of onion, the stalks (but not the leaves) of the parsley, a little salt and enough water to come halfway up the ingredients. Put a lid on the saucepan and simmer over very gentle heat for about four minutes or until the pieces of shellfish are just cooked. Remove the hard muscle from each scallop, which you will find opposite the orange roe.

Melt the butter in a saucepan and add the flour. Cook for thirty seconds, then draw off the heat and mix in the milk. Add five or six tablespoons of the stock in which the shellfish were cooked and stir steadily until boiling. You are aiming for a very thick but well-flavoured sauce. If the sauce seems too thin allow it to boil rapidly to reduce to the right consistency. If it is too thick add more milk or, if you have it, fish stock. Put back the shellfish, taste, and season with more salt if necessary.

Lay the eight French pancakes out on the table top and divide the mixture between them. Fold each up into a small square parcel. Using a pastry brush coat the whole parcel with beaten egg, paying particular attention to the joins.

Heat the oil in the deep-fryer until a crumb will sizzle vigorously in it. Lower the seafood envelopes into the hot oil and fry to a good golden brown. Drain on crumpled kitchen paper and serve at once. They go soggy if kept for any length of time.

A thin tomato sauce (recipe p. 14) is good with the dish, but by no means essential. A thick dusting of grated cheese is good too.

Deep-fried turbot and salmon kebab

This kebab is first coated in a light batter and then deep-fried in oil. Were it served with fine chipped straw potatoes it would be the most elegant version of fish and chips known to man. It must, of course, be cooked just before serving.

½ lb (225 g) turbot fillet, skinned
½ lb (225 g) fresh salmon
2 tablespoons cornflour
1 egg
Salt
A little water
Oil for deep frying

Cut the fish into fairly large cubes. Skewer them, turbot and salmon alternating, on four short skewers (preferably metal). Dip the whole kebabs in a batter made by mixing together the egg, the cornflour, a teaspoon of salt and enough water to give a thin cream.

Heat the fat until a crumb will sizzle vigorously in it, then make sure the kebabs are well coated in the batter. Fry the kebabs, taking care that they do not stick to each other in the fat. As soon as they are brown they will be cooked. Serve them as they are or with segments of lemon.

To serve:
Segments lemon (optional)

Serves 4

Deep-fried sole with almonds

The only snag about deep-frying is the smell of it that clings to hair and clothes. But this dish is so quick and delicious it is worth donning an overall and shower-cap over your dinner clothes.

1 lb (450 g) sole (or halibut, turbot, lemon sole or brill) fillet, skinned and cut into finger-length strips
2 egg whites
2 tablespoons cornflour
Salt
3 oz (85 g) flaked almonds
Wedges of lemon
Oil for deep frying

Serves 4

Beat the egg whites until frothy and mix with the cornflour. Mix this with the fish and the almonds. You will now have a rather sticky mass, with the sole pieces sticking together.

Heat the fat until a crumb will sizzle vigorously in it. Once it is hot, but not before, sprinkle half a teaspoon of salt into the fish and batter mixture, turning it well with your fingers. Lift the strips of sole one or two at a time from the bowl and drop them into the sizzling fat. With any luck the almonds will adhere to the fish, but do not worry if they float off. Once all the fish is in the fryer turn the temperature up and fry until the almonds are a medium brown and the fish pieces just beginning to colour – they should be very crisp and a pale gold. Drain the fish, and any drifting almonds on absorbent paper, then tip onto a hot serving dish. Serve with wedges of lemon as soon as you can. The batter will not stay crisp for more than four or five minutes so speed is essential.

61

Spinach timbale with seafood

The spinach timbale mixture may be prepared several hours in advance of cooking and the seafood mixture can be pre-cooked. But the baking of the timbale must be done immediately before dinner, and the seafood must be reheated carefully for fear of overcooking the ingredients. The mixture does not freeze successfully.

For the seafood mixture:
8 fresh or frozen scallops
1 lb (450 g) good white fish, e.g. haddock, cod or halibut, skinned
1 pint (570 ml) live mussels
½ lb (225 g) button mushrooms, sliced
1 or 2 shallots, finely chopped
¼ pint (150 ml) dry white wine
¼ pint (150 ml) water
¾ oz (20 g) butter
¾ oz (20 g) flour
3 tablespoons cream
Salt, pepper

For the spinach mould:
1½ lb (675 g) fresh spinach
1 oz (30 g) butter
3½ oz (100 g) fresh white breadcrumbs
12 fluid oz (345 ml) hot milk
2 eggs, beaten
1 egg yolk
Pinch ground nutmeg
Salt, freshly ground black pepper

Serves 4

Scrub the mussels vigorously in cold water, removing the beards. Tap each one on the side of the sink and if it will not close immediately, throw it away. Put the mussels into a large saucepan and add the wine and water. Cover with a good lid and put over moderate heat for four or five minutes or until all the mussels have opened. Do not throw away the liquid in the pan but lift out the mussels and remove them from their shells. Remove the 'rubber band' round each one and put the mussels in a bowl. Cover them to prevent drying out.

Cut the white fish into small pieces and put into a saucepan with the scallops (removed from their shells if fresh, with any liquid from the packet if frozen). Tip the wine and water from the mussel pan on top of the fish and scallops and cover with a lid.* Simmer gently for five or six minutes or until fish and scallops are cooked, but still tender. Lift out the scallops and carefully remove the tough piece of muscle found opposite the orange roe or coral. Cut each scallop into four and add to the mussels in the bowl, with the pieces of fish.

Melt the butter in a frying pan and in it gently fry the shallots until soft. Add the sliced mushrooms and fry briskly for two or three minutes. Stir in the flour and cook for a further thirty seconds. Draw the pan off the heat and strain on the liquid in which all the fish has been cooked. Stir until the sauce boils and thickens. Taste and add salt, pepper and cream. If the sauce is very thin boil it rapidly until it is of a creamy consistency. Pour this sauce over the seafood in the bowl and mix gently. Keep warm.

Now make the spinach mould mixture. Wash the spinach well, and remove the tough stalks. Put it still wet into a saucepan with a lid and, holding the pan in one hand and the lid on with the other, shake and toss the spinach at fairly high heat until it is soft and reduced in quantity. Drain well and remove fifteen of the best and biggest leaves. Drain these on absorbent paper. Squeeze all the water from the remaining spinach, pressing it between two plates. Tip onto a board and chop very finely. Butter a 6 in (15 cm) cake tin or soufflé dish and line it with the whole spinach leaves.

Melt the butter in a saucepan, add the spinach, and stir until very dry-looking. Take off the heat and add the breadcrumbs, beaten eggs, egg yolk, nutmeg and seasoning. Heat the milk and stir it into the mixture. Spoon the spinach mixture into the cake tin and cover with buttered foil.

Heat the oven to 180°C/350°F/Gas Mark 4. Stand the cake tin in a roasting pan full of boiling water. Bake in the oven for forty-five minutes or until the mixture is firm.

Turn out on a hot serving dish, and spoon the seafood mixture, and its sauce, over the top.

*There might still be a little sand from the mussels in the liquid. If there is, take care when pouring to leave it behind.

Scallops with chorizo

This dish used to be done at Leith's when one of our chefs was a Spaniard with a passion for seafood. Today it is only made for private parties because the price of fresh scallops has driven it off the regular table d'hôte menu. The baking must be done at the last minute, but the sausage and shallot can be fried in advance and the scallops prepared ready for the oven.

12 large fresh scallops
2 oz (55 g) Spanish
    chorizo sausage, sliced
2 shallots, finely chopped
A little olive oil
1 clove garlic, crushed
4 tablespoons fairly dry
    white breadcrumbs
1 tablespoon freshly
    grated Parmesan cheese

You will also need four
    scallop shells or small
    oven-proof dishes.

In a frying pan gently soften the chopped shallot in a little olive oil. Dice the sausage as finely as you can – the pieces should be not much bigger than those of the chopped shallot. Add them and the garlic to the shallot in the pan and turn up the heat until both the onion and sausage are just beginning to brown. Divide this mixture between the four scallop dishes and heat the grill. Set the oven at 200°C/400°F/Gas Mark 6.

Cut the tough muscle from each scallop. It is found opposite the orange roe. Put three scallops into each scallop dish and spoon a teaspoon of olive oil over each portion. Mix the grated cheese with the crumbs and scatter evenly over the top. About eight or ten minutes before serving put the dishes into the oven and cook until the scallops feel firm to the touch but still very tender (about seven minutes). Now quickly grill the scallops until the breadcrumbs are just beginning to brown, and serve at once.

Serves 4

Spinach roulade with hollandaise

The roulade mixture can be made several hours before baking but the egg whites should not be whipped and folded into it, nor the mixture baked until fifteen minutes or so before serving. The hollandaise sauce will keep at the right consistency for an hour if left in a bowl standing in a saucepan of hot water.

1 lb (450 g) fresh young spinach
½ oz (15 g) butter
Salt, freshly ground black pepper
Good grating fresh nutmeg
4 large eggs, separated
Cupful of water
1 tablespoon grated Parmesan cheese

For the filling:
½ oz (15 g) butter
½ lb (225 g) field mushrooms, finely sliced
1 clove garlic, crushed
½ oz (15 g) flour
⅓ pint (190 ml) milk
3 or 4 tablespoons cream
Salt, freshly ground black pepper

For the sauce:
2 egg yolks
1 tablespoon water
3 tablespoons wine vinegar
¼ lb (110 g) melted butter
Salt, pepper
½ bay leaf
6 peppercorns

Serves 4

First make the sauce. Pour the melted butter through a double J-cloth or muslin into a jug. Put the vinegar, bay leaf and peppercorns into a small shallow saucepan and boil vigorously until reduced to about a tablespoonful. Draw off the heat, lift out the peppercorns and bay leaf and add one tablespoon of cold water. This will cool the vinegar sufficiently to add the two egg yolks. Whisk the egg yolks into the vinegar and then put the pan back on a moderate heat. Whisk over the heat until the egg yolks look thick and fluffy and have risen slightly in the pan. Still whisking with one hand use the other to pour in the butter slowly, in a thin steady stream. You should whisk fast enough to incorporate the butter, and the sauce should gradually take on a creamy thick consistency. When all the butter is in, draw the pan off the heat and season with salt and pepper. Keep warm standing in a bowl of hot water.

Now make the spinach mixture. Remove the thick stalks from the spinach and wash the leaves thoroughly. Put into a large saucepan and add a cupful of water. Cover with a well-fitting lid. Shake the leaves, turning them frequently over a moderate heat until they are much reduced in bulk, soft and tender, but still bright green. Drain well and squeeze out all the moisture, either between two plates or in a cloth. Chop the spinach as finely as you can, or blend it in a liquidizer. Beat in the butter, season well with salt, freshly ground black pepper and a good grating of nutmeg.

Heat the oven to 190°C/375°F/Gas Mark 5. Before you add the eggs to the spinach mixture get the tin ready. Choose a very large roasting tin or a Swiss roll tin with a good lip. Line it with greaseproof paper and brush the paper with melted butter. Beat the four egg yolks into the spinach mixture and check the seasoning. You should have a fairly sloppy mixture. Using a wire whisk or an electric beater whisk the four egg whites until stiff but not dry-looking. Fold them into the spinach mixture, taking care not to overmix. Spread this in the Swiss roll tin and place in the oven. It will take about ten minutes to bake when it should feel dry and be slightly wrinkled at the edges.

To make the filling cook the chopped mushrooms in the butter for two or three minutes or until soft. Add the garlic and stir for a further half minute. Stir in the flour and then gradually stir in the milk. When the sauce boils stop stirring but allow it to simmer for thirty seconds or so. Stir in the cream, and season with salt and pepper.

Once the baking spinach mixture is ready loosen it from the sides of the tin. Put a large piece of greaseproof paper or foil on the table-top and sprinkle it with the grated Parmesan cheese. Turn the spinach cake upside-down onto this. Carefully peel off the backing paper. Spread the mushroom filling all over the spinach and roll up as you would a Swiss roll. Ease it onto a serving-dish and scatter a little more grated cheese on top if you like. Serve hot with the hollandaise sauce.

Spinach in cream

This is such a simple recipe we hesitate to include it, but it makes a wonderfully fresh starter to a dinner, or can be served as a vegetable.

2 lb (900 g) fresh young spinach
¼ pint (150 ml) double cream
1 oz (30 g) butter
Grated nutmeg
Squeeze lemon juice
Salt, freshly ground black pepper

Serves 4

Remove the spinach stalks and wash the leaves very well. Put them still wet but without any further water into a large saucepan with a well-fitting lid. Holding the saucepan in one hand and keeping the lid on with the other shake the spinach over a moderate heat until soft and reduced in bulk, but still bright green. Remove from the saucepan and tip onto a board. Mop up any of the excess moisture by pressing the spinach with absorbent paper or a tea towel (alternatively put the spinach between two plates and squeeze them together to force out the liquid).

Melt the butter in the dried-out saucepan and return the spinach to it. Toss the leaves in the butter until they are thoroughly coated, and season them with salt and plenty of black pepper. Tip them into a serving-dish, or into four individual serving-dishes. Season the double cream with a little salt, pepper, a good grating of fresh nutmeg and a squeeze of lemon juice. Spoon this over the spinach and serve at once.

Hot spinach with mushrooms

2 lb (900 g) fresh spinach
½ lb (225 g) black field
  mushrooms, sliced
1 shallot, finely chopped
2 oz (55 g) butter
1 carton soured cream
½ clove garlic, crushed
Salt, freshly ground black
  pepper
Grated nutmeg

Serves 4

Cook the spinach as described in the previous recipe for spinach in cream. Melt the butter in the dried-out saucepan and put the sliced mushrooms into it. Fry them for three or four minutes until browned at the edges and soft inside. Add the finely chopped shallot and cook for a further minute. Put back the now fairly dry spinach and mix it with the fried mushrooms. Add a few twists of the black peppermill, and season lightly with salt.

Tip into a warm serving-dish. Mix together the soured cream, crushed garlic, a good grating of fresh nutmeg, and salt and freshly ground black pepper. Spoon this over the spinach and serve at once.

Macaroni, cheese and mushroom pie

The next dish is too simple and inexpensive for most restaurant diners' tastes, but it is a dish we sometimes make to feed the staff at lunch time, and it is a great family favourite.
Freezes well. Thaw before re-heating.

½ lb (225 g) macaroni or
  other pasta
¾ lb (340 g) mushrooms,
  sliced
½ clove garlic, crushed
1½ oz (45 g) flour
1 pint (570 ml) milk
2½ oz (70 g) butter
3 oz (85 g) good strong
  grated cheese, any kind
Salt, black pepper
Pinch mustard
2 tablespoons white
  breadcrumbs, slightly
  stale

Serves 5 or 6

Boil the macaroni in plenty of salted water for ten minutes, stirring occasionally. Drain, and swish under the hot tap. Allow to dry off in a colander.

Melt the butter in a large saucepan. In it fry the mushrooms and garlic for three minutes. Stir in the flour, then the milk. Stir until boiling, then season with a little salt, plenty of black pepper and a pinch of mustard (or half a teaspoon made French mustard). Simmer until it is the consistency of double cream. Take off the heat, stir in all but a tablespoon of the cheese, then mix with the macaroni.

Tip into a pie dish, and scatter the crumbs and remaining cheese on top. Twenty minutes before serving put the dish into a hot oven to reheat, and to brown the top.

Seafood kebab with tarragon sauce

This is a very simple kebab, though hardly cheap. The sauce, which is a version of hollandaise, may be kept warm, standing in a bowl of hot water, for half an hour or so. The kebab must be cooked at the last minute.

4 large scallops
½ lb (225 g) raw scampi
½ lb (225 g) firm white
  fish, e.g. turbot or
  halibut, skinned
4 long thin rashers of
  streaky bacon
¼ lb (110 g) button
  mushrooms
Melted butter
Freshly ground black
  pepper

For the sauce:
2 tablespoons wine
  vinegar
5 or 6 peppercorns
½ bay leaf
1 tablespoon water
2 egg yolks
¼ lb (110 g) butter
1 tablespoon chopped
  tarragon
Pinch salt

Serves 4

Start with the sauce. Melt the butter carefully: it needs to be liquid but not hot. Then strain it through a piece of fine muslin, or through a double J-cloth, and pour it into a small jug.

Put the vinegar, peppercorns and bay leaf into a small saucepan, stand it over direct heat and allow the vinegar to boil until it is reduced to one tablespoon. With a perforated spoon lift out the peppercorns and bay leaf. Add the tablespoon of cold water to the vinegar in the pan and allow to cool for half a minute or so. Drop the yolks into the pan and with a fine wire whisk beat yolks and vinegar to a good froth. Put the pan over a moderate heat and whisk steadily until the mixture begins to mount up the pan, looking thick and frothy. Slowly pour a thin steady stream of melted butter into the egg yolk mixture, whisking all the time. When all the butter has been whisked in you should have a thick creamy emulsion. Add the tarragon and salt. To keep the sauce without allowing it to harden or to separate, stand it, still in the saucepan, in a bowl of hot water, while you make the kebabs.

Get the grill blazing hot. While it is heating remove the rind from the rashers of bacon and cut each rasher in two. Cut the skinned turbot or other white fish into eight neat cubes. Wrap each piece in a strip of bacon. If the scallops are fresh lift them from their shells. If either fresh or frozen and thawed remove the hard piece of muscle found opposite the pink coral. Cut each scallop in half. Dry the scampi, if they were frozen, on absorbent paper. Cut the mushrooms in half if they are large. Thread scallops, scampi, bacon-wrapped fish, and mushrooms onto four skewers. Brush them with a little melted butter, and grind black pepper all over them.

Grill the kebabs under as fierce a heat as possible, turning them frequently to get an even brown. As soon as the fish is cooked serve the kebabs with the tarragon sauce.

Baked gnocchi

Tomato sauce (recipe page 14) is good with gnocchi. Or a little cream can be poured over them before baking.

12 fl oz (345 ml) milk
2½ oz (70 g) semolina
1 oz (30 g) butter, melted
1 egg yolk
Small pinch nutmeg
Pinch salt
White pepper
2 tablespoons grated
    Parmesan cheese

Serves 4

Brush a flat tray, and an ovenproof flattish dish, with melted butter.

Bring the milk to a gentle boil, add the semolina, stir for three or four minutes. Remove from heat and stir in half the cheese, the egg yolk, nutmeg, and salt and pepper to taste. When the mixture is smooth, pour it into the greased flat tray and flatten by hand to the thickness of about ¾ inch (2 cm).

When cold, cut the gnocchi with a pastry cutter to form crescents, rings or whatever shape you fancy. Lay them in the greased ovenproof dish, and sprinkle with more melted butter and with the remaining Parmesan.

Place in a pre-heated oven (200°C/400°F/ Gas Mark 6) for ten to fifteen minutes or until golden. Serve immediately.

Moules marinières with a velvety cream sauce

This recipe is a glorified version of the French fisherman's mussel stew. It should be cooked and eaten within half an hour.

4 pints (2.28 l) or 4 lb (1.8 kg) live mussels
2 or 3 shallots, or 1 medium onion, very finely chopped
½ pint (290 ml) dry white wine
¾ oz (20 g) butter
¾ oz (20 g) flour
¼ pint (150 ml) double cream
1 tablespoon chopped parsley or chervil
Salt, pepper

Serves 4

Wash the mussels, scrubbing them well and pulling off the beards. Discard any mussels that refuse to close firmly when tapped on the side of the sink. Choose a large saucepan with a good fitting lid and put into it the chopped shallot or onion and the white wine. Tip in the mussels and put on the lid. Shake the pan gently, covered, over a moderate heat for three or four minutes or until all the mussels have opened. It may be necessary to stir and turn them halfway through the cooking process.

Once they are all opened lift them out of the juice and put them into a large serving-dish. Cover them with a piece of foil or a damp tea towel to stop them drying out. In a saucepan melt the butter and stir in the flour. Slowly whisk in the liquid from the mussel pan, and bring the sauce to the boil. Allow it to boil until reduced to about ⅓ pint (190 ml). Take off the heat, add salt and pepper to taste and just before serving add the chopped parsley or chervil and the cream. Reheat, pour all over the mussels and serve at once.

Gruyère and ham fondue

This is a last-minute dish, but it can be cooked at the table if you have a heavy fondue pot.

¾ lb (340 g) grated Gruyère cheese
1 small clove garlic
½ oz (15 g) butter
3 fluid oz (85 ml) dry white wine
Dash of Kirsch
3 turns of the peppermill
2 oz (55 g) chopped cooked ham

To serve:
4 large slices of toast cut into finger-thin pieces

Serves 4

Melt the butter in a thick pan or enamelled cast iron one. Bruise the garlic slightly, then fry it for thirty seconds in the butter. Add the white wine and bring to the boil. Then, using a wooden spoon, stir in the grated cheese 1 oz (30 g) at a time until it softens and melts, and all the cheese is used up. Do not boil, but keep near boiling point. The mixture should be like a thick white sauce. Remove the garlic clove. Finish with pepper, Kirsch and chopped ham.

If a fondue pot is not used the pan can be brought to the table and kept hot with a spirit lamp, or the fondue can be poured into small heated ramekin dishes and served individually. Each guest dips his toast strips into the cheese fondue and eats with his fingers or a fork.

Deep-fried Gruyère and chicken pancakes

This variation of a Turkish Beureck can be made with left-over chicken. The pancakes can be stuffed and ready for deep-frying, then kept a day in the refrigerator, or longer if frozen. They may be deep-fried straight from the freezer but an extra two minutes' frying time should be allowed to ensure that the filling reheats thoroughly.

½ lb (225 g) cooked
   chicken flesh
¼ lb (110 g) Gruyère
   cheese
8 French pancakes
   (recipe p. 73)

For the suprème sauce:
½ oz (15 g) butter
4 fluid oz (110 ml) chicken
   stock
½ oz (15 g) plain flour
2 tablespoons double
   cream
Salt, white ground pepper
Pinch grated nutmeg

For the coating:
Plain flour
1 egg plus 1 egg white
2 tablespoons water
Pinch salt
Dried white breadcrumbs

Oil for deep frying

Serves 4

Melt the butter in a saucepan, add the flour, and stir for half a minute. Add the cold chicken stock and whisk to prevent lumps forming. Heat gently until the sauce thickens evenly, and boils. Add the double cream, and season with nutmeg, salt and pepper to taste. Simmer briefly, then allow to cool. Set aside.

Dice the cooked chicken and the Gruyère. Mix with the cold sauce suprème. Divide the mixture between the eight pancakes placing a tablespoon of filling in the centre of each. Fold the sides to enclose the filling completely. Beat the egg, egg white, water and pinch of salt together. Roll the stuffed pancakes first in plain flour, then dip them in the beaten egg, and finally roll them all over in breadcrumbs.

Heat deep fat or oil until a crumb will sizzle in it. Do not overheat the oil because the Beurecks would darken, before becoming soft and hot in the centre. Gently lower the breaded Beurecks a few at a time into the hot oil. Fry until golden, then drain well on absorbent kitchen paper. Repeat until all the pancakes are fried. Serve immediately.

Camembert fritters

Although this is a good way of using up under-ripe, or perhaps *slightly* over-ripe Camembert, the fritters are best made with perfect cheese. One Camembert will serve four people.

Sprigs of parsley (which must be dry, not recently washed), dropped into the hot fat until crisp and very bright green, are delicious with the fritters. They must be well drained of the frying fat.

Camembert
Fine white stale
   breadcrumbs
Beaten egg
Oil for deep frying

Chill the Camembert well, then cut it into small wedges. (If using the cheese ready wrapped in wedges, cut each wedge in half.) Roll the pieces of cheese first in beaten egg and then in very fine white breadcrumbs. Keep refrigerated until needed. Heat the oil until a crumb will sizzle vigorously in it. Fry the Camembert pieces in the hot fat until crisp and pale brown. Drain on absorbent kitchen paper and serve at once.

To serve:
Deep-fried parsley sprigs (optional)

Hot spicy sausage with potato

The potatoes for this recipe can be boiled in advance, and the French dressing made. But they should not be put together and reheated until just before serving.

About 3 oz (85 g) spicy
   garlic sausage (French
   or German is best)
1 lb (450 g) small waxy
   potatoes, peeled

For the French dressing:
4 tablespoons salad oil
1 tablespoon wine vinegar
½ clove garlic, crushed
1 tablespoon chopped
   parsley
Salt, freshly ground black
   pepper

Wrap the sausage in foil and heat it in the oven. Or steam it briefly.

Boil the potatoes in salted water until just tender. Drain and slice fairly thickly into four shallow hot oven-proof dishes. Peel and slice the hot sausage. Lay the sausage slices on top of the hot potato.

For the French dressing mix the oil, vinegar, garlic and chopped parsley together, and season well with salt and plenty of freshly ground black pepper. Pour this dressing all over the potatoes and sausage and serve at once.

Serves 4

71

Seafood and spinach soufflé

Another spinach and seafood dish, not unlike that on p. 62, but fluffier.

More substantial than the classic soufflé, this dish does well for lunch or supper. The seafood mixture and the egg and spinach mixture may be made in advance but the whisking of the egg whites and the baking must be done at the last minute.

½ lb (225 g) fillet cod, skinned and cut into cubes
4 scallops (in their shells when available: if not, frozen)
½ lb (225 g) raw scampi
6 oz (170 g) peeled cooked prawns
1 lb (450 g) spinach
3 tablespoons double cream
2 eggs
8 fluid oz (235 ml) white wine
The white part of one large leek
2 oz (55 g) butter
1 oz (30 g) flour
Salt, pepper
Grated nutmeg

Serves 4

Wash the spinach. Cook briefly in a cupful of salted water until reduced in quantity, and bright green. Cool under the cold water tap and drain thoroughly, pressing out all the moisture you can. Chop finely and reserve a quarter of it for the soufflé. Lay the remaining part on an oven-proof dish, with a good lip. Season with salt, pepper and grated nutmeg.

For the seafood mixture, shred the leek into fine matchstick 'julienne' strips. Melt half the butter in a frying pan and gently cook the julienne of leek until soft. Remove the hard muscle from the scallops (found opposite the roe). Add the cod and all the seafood, pour in the white wine, and season with salt and pepper. Simmer slowly for three minutes. Lift out the seafood with a perforated spoon and put on top of the spinach bed. Keep the wine simmering. Add the cream and check the seasoning.

Heat the oven to 220°C/425°F/Gas Mark 7. Melt the remaining ounce of butter in a stew-pan, stir in the flour and cook for a minute. Draw the pan off the heat and gradually blend in the hot wine and cream. Stir until boiling, then pour two tablespoons of this sauce over the seafood. Cool the remaining sauce slightly, then beat in the egg yolks and the remaining chopped spinach. Keep warm.

Beat the whites of the eggs until stiff but not dry. Fold them into the sauce and spoon the mixture over the seafood. Place in the pre-heated oven for fifteen to twenty minutes (less for a shallow dish, more for a deep one). Serve when raised and golden.

Scallop shells or ramekins could be used as individual cooking-cum-serving dishes, and would not need more than twelve minutes in the oven.

French pancakes

Pancakes freeze well: put them between layers of paper or plastic.

¼ lb (110 g) plain flour
1 tablespoon oil
1 large whole egg, plus 1 egg yolk
½ pint (290 ml) water or milk, or a mixture
½ teaspoon salt
A little butter or oil for frying

If you have a liquidizer or food processer, making the batter is child's play: simply put the egg and yolk, oil and liquid into it, whizz briefly and spoon in the flour, with the machine in motion. Don't overdo it or the batter will be too bubbly and frothy for use. Add the salt.

If making the mixture by hand put the flour and salt into a large mixing bowl and make a well in the centre. Drop the eggs into the middle and, using a wooden spoon, stir them together, gradually incorporating the surrounding flour. When the central paste becomes rather thick begin to add the water or milk so that the batter is again thinned to a manageable consistency. When all the flour is incorporated add any remaining liquid and mix until quite smooth.

Leave the batter to settle for at least thirty minutes before using. Wipe out an omelette pan or frying pan with a screw of kitchen paper dipped in cooking oil or melted butter. Resign yourself to the first pancake being a disaster: take a small ladleful of the batter mixture and pour it into the hot pan, tilting the pan so that the batter runs evenly all over the surface. Fry the pancake until a good brown underneath (lift an edge with a palette knife or fish slice to take a look). Once brown, flip the pancake over with the fish slice and fry the other side. The ideal pancake is wafer-thin and well browned. It is better to have the pancake batter on the thin side, risking a few lace-like holes, than having a thick batter which would produce doughy pancakes.

As the pancakes are made put them on a plate and keep them covered with a tea towel. They can be reheated in the oven, loosely covered with foil.

Stuffed eggplant

This recipe is excellent for using up left-over roast lamb. It is best eaten straight from the oven, and should not be frozen.

2 small round eggplants (aubergines)
2 tablespoons olive oil
¼ lb (110 g) onions, chopped
2 cloves garlic
2 large tomatoes, peeled and chopped
1 tablespoon tomato purée
1 pinch dried thyme (or 1 teaspoon fresh, chopped)
1 bay leaf
2 pinches dried oregano (or 1 teaspoon chopped or fresh marjoram)
6 oz (170 g) lean cooked lamb, minced
Salt, pepper
2 oz (55 g) Gruyère cheese, grated

Serves 4

Cut the eggplants in half lengthwise. Using a small knife deeply score the flesh, taking care not to pierce the skin. Heat a tablespoon of olive oil in a frying pan and gently fry the aubergines flat side down. Turn over and fry the skin side too. This will help to remove the pulp. Allow to cool. Using the same pan and more olive oil, gently fry the chopped onions until soft, then add the garlic and fry for half a minute more.

Carefully remove the pulp from the aubergine shells and chop it coarsely. Add to the onion pan with the chopped tomatoes, tomato purée, thyme, bay leaf, oregano, lamb, salt and pepper. Allow to simmer until the tomato liquid has mostly evaporated, leaving a thick mixture. Check the seasoning. Divide the mixture between the empty shells. Sprinkle with the grated cheese and reheat in a hot oven, 230°C/450°F/Gas Mark 8, until the cheese is melted and bubbling.

Fish

Quenelles

Salmon quenelles with Chablis cream sauce

Quenelles are said to be difficult. A child could make these, and they are unfailingly good. They will freeze if well coated with sauce, but are fractionally better freshly cooked. The quenelle mixture can be made four or five hours in advance, as can the sauce. This leaves only the final poaching to be coped with just before dinner, and that is very quick.

For the quenelles:
1 lb (450 g) salmon fillet, skinned and de-boned
¼ lb (225 g) whiting fillet, skinned and de-boned
4 slices white bread without the crusts
1 cup milk
2 egg whites
Salt, white pepper
Pinch cayenne pepper
Up to ¾ pint (425 ml) double cream

For the poaching liquid:
2 pints (good litre) water
Glass dry white wine
2 tablespoons vinegar
5 or 6 parsley stalks
A few slices onion
1 bay leaf
The skins and bones from the fish and any extra fish heads or trimmings

First make the poaching liquid by combining the ingredients and simmering for twenty minutes. Strain the liquid into a shallow saucepan.

Now make the quenelles. Mince the salmon and whiting flesh twice so that it is a fine paste. Soak the bread in the milk, squeezing out any excess so that you have damp but not soggy bread. Put the bread in a mixing machine if you have one and slowly beat the fish flesh into it. In the absence of a machine use a pestle and mortar or a bowl and a wooden spoon. Season the mixture with the peppers only. Beat the egg whites until just frothy, then slowly work them into the fish paste. When all the whites are incorporated put the mixture into the refrigerator and forget about it until half an hour before serving.

Meanwhile make the sauce. Put ½ pint (290 ml) of the poaching liquid and the ¼ pint (150 ml) of Chablis in a saucepan and boil rapidly until reduced to ½ pint (290 ml) in total. In a second saucepan melt half the butter and stir in the flour. Draw off the heat and gradually beat in the ½ pint (290 ml) of wine and fish stock mixture. Return to the heat and stir until boiling. Simmer for ten minutes or so, or until the sauce is reduced to a thickish syrupy consistency. Slowly whisk in the remaining butter, bit by bit. Stir in the cream and taste for seasoning, adding salt and white pepper as necessary. Cover the sauce and set aside for reheating later.

Take the chilled quenelle mixture out of the fridge and gradually beat as much double cream into it as it will hold. This will be at least 8 fluid oz (235 ml) and may be as much as ¾ pint (425 ml). You should end up with a mixture that will just hold its shape and that drops reluctantly off the spoon when the spoon is given a slight jerk. Season with salt. Taste the

For the sauce:
¼ pint (150 ml) Chablis
  or other dry white wine
4 tablespoons double
  cream
2 oz (55 g) butter
¾ oz (20 g) flour
Salt, white pepper

Serves 4–6

mixture (it is most important that the seasoning is right; and, surprisingly, raw fish tastes
fine).

Heat the poaching liquid in the shallow
saucepan, and add boiling water if it is less
than 1 in (2½ cm) deep. Using two dessert-
spoons dipped in hot water (or into the
poaching liquid) form the quenelle mixture
into egg shapes and slip them one by one into
the poaching liquid. They will sink.

The quenelles will take between five and
twelve minutes to cook, depending on their
size. They are done when they will float, and
feel firm to the touch. To test, fish one out, cut
it open and try it. When the quenelles are
done lift them out of the liquid with a perforated
spoon and put them into a serving-dish. Reheat
the sauce carefully without boiling it and spoon
over the quenelles. Serve at once.

Scallop quenelles with lobster sauce

Follow the salmon
quenelles recipe (p. 77)
but substitute the sauce
below and replace the
salmon with fresh or
frozen (but thawed)
scallops. The whiting is
essential.

For the sauce:
1 tin lobster bisque
1 tablespoon brandy
¼ pint (150 ml) double
  cream
Pinch cayenne
Salt, pepper

Serves 4–6

To make the sauce mix together all the sauce
ingredients with enough of the poaching liquid
to give a creamy consistency. Heat without
boiling and pour over the quenelles.

Turbot quenelles with mussel sauce

These are made like salmon quenelles (recipe p. 77) but are served with a different sauce. 1 lb (450 g) of turbot flesh replaces the salmon.

For the sauce:
¼ pint (150 ml) double
  cream
1 can mussel soup
1 dessertspoon sherry
A little chopped fresh dill
Salt, pepper

Serves 4–6

Proceed as for the salmon quenelles.

To make the sauce, combine the mussel soup, the cream, sherry and enough of the poaching liquid to give a creamy consistency. Add the chopped dill and salt and pepper to taste. Pour over the quenelles and serve.

Pike quenelles with scallop sauce

Follow the salmon quenelles recipe (p. 77) omitting the sauce and substituting 1½ lb (675 g) of pike fillet for the salmon and the whiting. The scallops may be replaced by scampi, prawns or any other seafood.

For the sauce:
¼ pint (150 ml) white
  wine
4 tablespoons double
  cream
3 fresh scallops, taken
  from their shells
1 tin mussel soup

Serves 4–6

Proceed as for salmon quenelles. Then make the sauce. Remove the muscle from each scallop (found opposite the roe). Cut the scallops into small pieces, then put them with the wine into a saucepan. Heat until the wine is almost simmering, then allow to poach for two or three minutes or until the scallops are cooked. Lift the scallops out and put them aside for the moment. Boil the liquid rapidly for eight or ten minutes or until the wine has lost its strong alcoholic flavour. Add the soup and the cream. Put back the scallops. Spoon over the quenelles.

If fresh mussels are used rather than a tin of soup they could be cooked as described in the moules marinières recipe (p. 69). Their cooking juices, topped up to ½ pint (290 ml) with some of the quenelle poaching liquid, will need to be thickened with *beurre manié*: knead together ¾ oz (20 g) of butter and ¾ oz (20 g) of flour and drop this into the liquid, bit by bit, whisking all the time. When all the beurre manié is in the sauce it should be of the right consistency. At this stage put in the cooked mussels (taken from their shells) and scallops or other seafood.

Salmon

Poached salmon with burnt hollandaise

The title of this recipe is a slight misnomer. The hollandaise-covered fish is browned under the grill until dark but not truly burnt. The flavour is amazing – very nutty and buttery. I think it a great improvement on hollandaise sauce simply spooned over fish. The coating of the fish and the browning under the grill needs to be done pretty much at the last moment. It will not freeze.

Hollandaise sauce (recipe p. 13)
2–3 tablespoons double cream
4 pieces fresh salmon, either steaks or thin slices cut lengthways along the fish as one would for smoked salmon, only thicker

For the poaching liquid:
1 pint (570 ml) water
¼ pint (150 ml) vinegar
2 or 3 slices onion
1 stick celery
1 bay leaf
Sprig of thyme
1 tablespoon oil
6 peppercorns
1 teaspoon salt

Serves 4

Put all the ingredients for the poaching liquid into a deep wide frying pan or shallow saucepan and bring to the boil. Simmer for twenty minutes, then cool slowly. Carefully lower the fish into it, and poach, with the water barely moving, until the fish is cooked – about five minutes for ½ in (1 cm) steaks, two or three minutes for thin slices. Turn the grill to maximum.

Mix the double cream into the hollandaise sauce. Put the fish slices, as well drained as possible, onto a heat-proof serving-dish. Spoon the hollandaise cream all over the fish. Place at once under the blazing hot grill to brown the top. Serve promptly.

Poached salmon with sorrel sauce

Sorrel has a tart lemony flavour, particularly suitable for fish. Care should be taken not to cook the sorrel too long for fear of losing the pretty green colour, which quickly becomes an unattractive khaki if kept hot for long. The dish freezes well if the fish is well covered in the sauce but should not remain frozen for more than a week, for the sorrel gradually loses its colour.

4 thin slices salmon, cut as for smoked salmon, but thicker, and each weighing about 4–5 oz (110–140 g)

For the stuffing:
2 oz (55 g) button mushrooms, finely chopped
½ oz (15 g) butter
2 oz (55 g) peeled cooked prawns, finely chopped
1 tablespoon double cream
1 sprig dill, finely chopped
1 tablespoon white breadcrumbs
Salt, pepper

For the poaching liquid:
¼ pint (150 ml) white wine
½ pint (290 ml) water
2 or 3 slices onion
1 or 2 pieces celery
½ bay leaf
Few parsley stalks
1 teaspoon salt
6 peppercorns

First of all make the stuffing. Fry the chopped mushroom in the butter for two minutes, then mix with the crumbs, prawns, cream and the chopped dill. Season with salt and pepper. Lay the four salmon slices out on a board and spread the stuffing mixture on them. Roll them up and tuck them, side by side, into a small oven-proof dish.

Boil together all the poaching liquid ingredients for twenty minutes. Strain this over the fish and poach (covered) in a moderate oven (190°C/375°F/Gas Mark 5) for twelve or fifteen minutes or until the salmon feels firm to the touch. Alternatively the salmon rolls may be poached in a covered frying pan on the top of the cooker, in which case the cooking time should be eight to ten minutes.

Using a perforated spoon or fish slice lift the salmon rolls onto a serving-dish. Do not throw away the cooking liquid. Cover the salmon with a piece of foil or a lid to prevent drying out while you make the sauce.

Melt half the butter in a saucepan and stir in the flour. Stir over a moderate heat for thirty seconds, then strain on the liquid in which the fish was cooked. Put back over the heat and stir until boiling. The sauce should be of about the consistency of thin cream. If it is too thin boil it rapidly to reduce it to the correct consistency. Taste and add salt and pepper as necessary. Just before serving beat in the remaining butter, bit by bit. Then stir in the cream and add the finely chopped sorrel. Pour over the fish and serve at once.

For the sauce:
¾ oz (20 g) butter
1 teaspoon flour
5 young sorrel leaves, washed and very finely chopped
2 tablespoons cream
Salt, pepper

Serves 4

81

Trout

Sea trout in a foil case

Few people realize that the delicate expensive sea trout with its pale salmon-like colour and fresh creamy taste is in fact the same animal as that boring trout raised on the average fish farm. Happily, however, there are some fish farmers now producing fish on a diet similar to that which their brothers are eating in the sea. This gives them their beautiful pink colour, firm flesh and good taste. If you are lucky enough to get hold of a 2–3 lb (900 g–1.35 kg) trout like this the simplest and best way to cook it is as follows.

Put the thoroughly cleaned trout whole onto a large piece of buttered foil. Brush the top of the fish with butter and grind plenty of black pepper all over it. Squeeze half a lemon over it too, and tuck the empty lemon shell into the body cavity. Add a few herbs if you like them (dill, tarragon, fennel are particularly good) and sprinkle two to three tablespoons white wine on top. Wrap up the fish, taking care that there are no holes in the foil for the juice to leak out.

Put the fish into the oven and bake it until a skewer will glide easily right through foil parcel, fish and all. This will take about twenty minutes for a 2 lb (900 g) fish in a hot oven, half an hour in a moderate oven and three-quarters of an hour for a medium-sized fish (3 or 4 lb (1.35 or 1.8 kg)) in a moderate oven. Largish fish should not be cooked in a too-fierce oven.

Once the fish is done take it out very carefully, making sure that you do not lose any of the juices, and dish it on a large fireproof platter. Put it under a hot grill to brown and blister the top skin, pour over the juices from the foil package and serve at once.

Poached trout with cream and fennel sauce

If the trout is really fresh when cooked this dish will freeze satisfactorily. Take care that the fish are completely covered in the sauce when put in the freezer.

4 river trout, cleaned
¼ lb (110 g) fennel, finely cut into *julienne* (or matchstick) strips
1½ oz (45 g) butter
8 fluid oz (235 ml) dry white wine
4 fluid oz (110 ml) water or fish stock
Pinch aniseed powder, or dried fennel powder
2 oz (55 g) shallots or onions, finely chopped
Salt, freshly ground white pepper
¾ oz (20 g) plain flour
¼ pint (150 ml) double cream

Heat the oven to 220°C/425°F/Gas Mark 7. Smear a fireproof dish with ½ oz (15 g) butter, sprinkle the bottom with the chopped shallots or onions and lay the trout in it. Season with salt and pepper. Add the wine and the water or fish stock. Cover with foil and bake for ten to fifteen minutes. Remove from the oven, and lift the fish out onto a serving dish. Remove the skin carefully, cover the fish with foil and keep warm. Reduce the cooking stock by rapid boiling until you have about ⅓ pint (190 ml). Skim off any froth.

Heat 1 oz (30 g) of butter in a small stewpan and gently cook the fennel *julienne* until soft. Stir in the flour. Mix well, then strain on the reduced cooking liquid. Stir until boiling. Add the cream and the aniseed or fennel powder. Check the seasoning and simmer for a few minutes. Spoon over the trout and serve.

Serves 4

Trout in rosé wine sauce

Like the poached trout in the recipe above this dish will freeze satisfactorily if the trout is really fresh when cooked. Trout that is a day or two old, or has been frozen before, does not freeze well – it loses any firmness it once had, becoming mushy rather than tender.

4 river trout, cleaned
About 1 oz (30 g) butter
2 shallots, chopped
½ lb (225 g) white
  mushrooms, sliced
½ pint (290 ml) Provençe
  or Portuguese rosé
  wine
¾ oz (20 g) flour
Salt, pepper
5 tablespoons double
  cream

Heat the oven to 220°C/425°F/Gas Mark 7. Smear the bottom of an ovenproof dish with a teaspoon of the butter, sprinkle with the chopped shallots and the sliced mushrooms. Lay the fish on top and season with salt and pepper. Pour over the rosé wine, cover with a lid or a sheet of foil, and cook in the oven for twenty to twenty-five minutes, or until the fish feel firm to the touch. Lift the trout onto a serving-dish, peel off the skins and keep the fish covered and warm.

Reduce the cooking liquid (with the shallot and mushrooms) by rapid boiling until you have about ⅓ pint (190 ml). Melt ¾ oz (20 g) butter, stir in the flour and cook for thirty seconds. Draw the pan off the heat, blend in the cooking liquid and, stirring, bring to the boil. Add the cream, check the seasoning and pour over the fish.

Serves 4

Trout in oatmeal with lemon butter

This is a simple dish but very delicious. It requires, however, a prodigious amount of butter.

4 small trout, cleaned
A little flour
Beaten egg
Coarse oatmeal
Butter for frying
Juice of ½ lemon
Salt, freshly ground black
  pepper

To serve:
Lemon wedges (optional)

Serves 4

Split the trout open right down the belly. Take off the heads and open the trout flat on the chopping board, inside-down. Press along the backbone with the heel of your hand to loosen it. Then turn the fish over and carefully ease out the backbone bringing with it as many of the small side-bones as possible. Wash the trout and pat dry on absorbent kitchen paper or a clean tea towel. Season with salt and pepper. Close the trout up again so that they resume their original shape and dust them lightly with flour. Brush them with beaten egg and then press into the oatmeal so that they are well coated.

Melt 2 or 3 oz (55 or 85 g) of butter in a wide shallow frying pan and fry the fish on both sides, until the oatmeal is a good brown and the fish are tender when pierced with a skewer. They will need careful handling because the oatmeal is inclined to flake off, and they may

84

take as much as fifteen minutes to be cooked through. Add more butter as necessary.

When the fish are cooked dish them on a serving-platter and put another tablespoon of butter into the frying pan. Add the lemon juice and boil up until foaming. Pour immediately over the trout and serve at once, with a few lemon wedges if liked.

Wine lovers' trout

This recipe calls for fish stock, so a few fish heads and bones (any kind) must be begged from the fishmonger. Simply boil the heads, skin and bones in water with a few slices of onion and a bay leaf for twenty minutes, then strain. Boil again until reduced to 3 fluid oz (85 ml).

4 river trout, cleaned
3 fluid oz (85 ml) white wine
3 fluid oz (85 ml) red wine
3 fluid oz (85 ml) good fish stock
1 medium onion, chopped
3 fluid oz (85 ml) double cream
About 2½ oz (70 g) butter
Salt, pepper
1 oz (30 g) flour
2 oz (55 g) mushrooms, sliced

Heat the oven to 220°C/425°F/Gas Mark 7.

Use ½ oz (15 g) of the butter to grease the bottom of a roasting tin or ovenproof dish, sprinkle half the chopped onion all over it, add the sliced mushrooms and lay the trout on top. Sprinkle with salt and pepper. Pour the white wine in the dish, and cover with foil. Bake for ten to twenty minutes (the thinner the dish, the sooner it will start simmering) or until the fish feel firm. Remove.

To make the red wine sauce, gently fry the other half of the chopped onion in 1 oz (30 g) of the butter. When soft stir in half the flour (one heaped teaspoon). Add the cold red wine and the fish stock. Mix well. Gently simmer for ten minutes. Add salt and pepper to taste.

To make the white wine sauce, melt the remaining 1 oz (30 g) of butter, add the remaining ½ oz (15 g) of flour, then stir in the strained cooking liquid from poaching the fish, and add the cream. Taste and add salt and pepper. Simmer for two minutes. Divide the cooked mushrooms between the two sauces.

Remove the skin from the trout. Lay the fish in an oval serving-dish and spoon the red wine sauce over it down one side of the dish and the white wine sauce down the other. Serve immediately.

Serves 4

More Fish Recipes

Lemon sole fillets stuffed with salmon and herb mousse

This is a sophisticated dish, but is surprisingly easy to make. It is frequently served with little crescents of puff pastry (*fleurons*) (p. 91): the crispness of the hot pastry makes a delicious contrast to the soft creaminess of the fish. The dish will freeze satisfactorily, but it is best to serve it fresh from the oven. If it must be frozen make sure the fish is well coated with sauce, and thaw it before reheating.

8 small skinned fillets
  lemon sole
1 lb (450 g) fresh salmon,
  thinly sliced as for
  smoked salmon
1 tablespoon brandy
8 fluid oz (235 ml) white
  wine

For the herb stuffing:
1 lb (450 g) pike or
  whiting
1 tablespoon each
  chopped parsley,
  chives and tarragon
¼ pint (150 ml) double
  cream

First make the herb stuffing. Mince the whiting or pike flesh twice so that you have a fine paste. Soak the bread in the milk, then squeeze out any excess so that it is damp but not soggy. Put the bread in a mixing machine if you have one and slowly beat the fish flesh into it. In the absence of a machine use a pestle and mortar or a bowl and a wooden spoon. Season the mixture with pepper only. Beat the egg white until just frothy and then work into the fish paste. Chill the mixture for fifteen minutes or so and then beat the double cream into it, spoon by spoon, until you have a mixture that will just hold its shape and that drops reluctantly off the spoon when given a slight jerk. Season with salt and cayenne pepper, and beat in all the chopped herbs.

Lay the lemon sole fillets flat on the work top and cover them with a thick layer of the herby mixture. Then lay a thin salmon slice on the top of each fillet. Fold or roll the fillets so that they look like neat parcels and tuck them side by side into a buttered fireproof shallow dish. Pour over the wine, the brandy and, if you have them, tuck the stalks from the parsley and tarragon into the liquid. Season with salt and pepper and cover with a lid or foil. Cook at 220°C/425°F/Gas Mark 7 for fifteen to twenty minutes or until the fish parcels feel firm to the touch, and a skewer will glide easily into them. Lift them out and put them on a serving-dish. Cover tightly and keep warm.

To make the sauce, strain the liquid in which you have cooked the fish into a saucepan and boil it rapidly until it measures about 8 fluid

Salt, white pepper, pinch
  cayenne
2 slices white bread
  without the crusts
A little milk
1 egg white

For the sauce:
4 tablespoons double
  cream
2 oz (55 g) butter
¾ oz (20 g) flour
Salt, pepper

oz (235 ml). Melt half the butter and stir in
the flour. Cook for half a minute, then draw
the pan off the heat. Pour on the reduced
cooking liquor and blend in smoothly. Return
the pan to the heat and stir until you have a
thick sauce. Add the double cream, reheat and
then slowly whisk in the rest of the butter, bit
by bit. Add salt and pepper to taste and pour
over the lemon sole fillets.

Serves 4

Halibut steak with prawns, mushrooms and lemon butter

This is a remarkably
simple dish to do and
keeps well for an hour or
so in a very low oven if
covered with foil.

Butter for frying
1 small onion, very finely
  chopped
¼ lb (110 g) cooked peeled
  prawns
½ lb (225 g) button
  mushrooms, finely
  sliced
Lemon juice
1 tablespoon chopped
  parsley
Black pepper, salt
4 halibut steaks
A little flour

Serves 4

Wash the steaks well and pat them dry with a
clean tea towel or absorbent kitchen paper.
Dust them lightly on both sides with flour.
Heat a good tablespoon of butter in a frying
pan and when it is foaming lay in the steaks.
Shake the pan gently to prevent them sticking
and fry for about three minutes on each side or
until brown and fairly firm to the touch. Carefully lift out the steaks with a fish slice and dish
them on a serving plate, removing the skin as
you do so. Cover them with a piece of foil and
keep warm.

Melt another lump of butter in the same
frying pan and in it soften the chopped
onion until it is transparent. Add the button
mushrooms and turn up the heat. Fry fairly
fast for two minutes. Add the peeled prawns,
a good squeeze of lemon juice, a little more
butter if necessary and the chopped parsley.
Shake and stir over the heat until everything
is hot. Spoon this mixture neatly over the
steaks and season with a little salt and a good
grinding of fresh black pepper.

Creamy seafood pie

This recipe is particularly impressive if small individual pies can be contrived rather than one big family one. However, it must be admitted that the big one tastes exactly like the little ones. It is marginally better if made freshly, but will freeze well with the filling made but the pastry top unbaked. Thaw before baking.

¾ lb (340 g) puff pastry (frozen is fine, or see recipe p. 90)
8 fresh or frozen scallops
1 lb (450 g) good white fish, e.g. haddock, cod or halibut, skinned
1 pint (570 ml) live mussels
½ lb (225 g) button mushrooms, sliced
1 or 2 shallots, finely chopped
¼ pint (150 ml) dry white wine
¼ pint (150 ml) water
¾ oz (85 g) butter
¾ oz (85 g) flour
Salt, pepper
3 tablespoons cream
Beaten egg

Serves 4

*There might still be a little sand from the mussels in the liquid. If there is, take care when pouring to leave it behind.

Start with the mussels. Scrub them vigorously in cold water, removing the beards. Tap each one on the side of the sink and if it will not close immediately throw it away. Put the mussels in a large saucepan and add the wine and water. Cover with a good lid and put over moderate heat for four or five minutes or until all the mussels have opened. Do not throw away the liquid in the pan but lift out the mussels and remove them from their shells. Remove the 'rubber band' round each one and put the mussels in a bowl. Cover them to prevent them drying out. Discard the shells.

Put the white fish (skinned and cut into small pieces) in a saucepan with the scallops (removed from their shells if fresh, with any liquid from the packet if frozen). Tip the wine and water from the mussel pan on top of the fish and scallops and cover with a lid. Simmer gently for five or six minutes or until fish and scallops are cooked, but still tender. Lift out the scallops and remove the tough piece of muscle found opposite the orange roe or coral. Cut each scallop into four and add to the mussels and pieces of fish in the bowl.

Melt the butter in a frying pan, add the sliced mushrooms and fry briskly for two or three minutes. Stir in the flour and cook for a further thirty seconds. Draw the pan off the heat and strain on the liquid in which all the fish has been cooked.* Stir until the sauce boils and thickens. Taste and add salt and pepper as necessary. Stir in the cream. If the sauce is very thin boil it rapidly until it is of a creamy consistency. Pour this sauce over the seafood in the bowl and mix gently. Divide the mixture between four largish ramekin dishes or put into one medium-sized piedish. Allow to get quite cold.

Roll the pastry out very thinly and use it to cover the pie. Use any trimmings to decorate it elaborately. Little fish swimming about the pastry crust are pretty and amusing. Brush all over with beaten egg. Set the oven at 230°C/450°F/Gas Mark 8. Once it is blazing hot put in the pie or pies. When the pastry is well browned and puffed up the filling should be hot. The individual pies will take about twelve minutes, the large one, twenty.

Seafood vol-au-vent

¾ lb (340 g) puff pastry or
   one family-sized
   vol-au-vent
or
1 lb (450 g) for 4 smaller
   bouchée (frozen pastry
   is fine or see recipe
   p.90)

8 fresh or frozen scallops
1 lb (450 g) good white
   fish, e.g. haddock, cod
   or halibut, skinned
1 pint (570 ml) live
   mussels
½ lb (225 g) button
   mushrooms, sliced
1 or 2 shallots, finely
   chopped
¼ pint (150 ml) dry white
   wine
¼ pint (150 ml) water
¾ oz (85 g) butter
¾ oz (85 g) flour
Salt, pepper
3 tablespoons cream
Beaten egg

This recipe is almost identical to the seafood pie above, varying only in the presentation. Small bouchée cases (individual one-portion size cases) or one larger vol-au-vent case can be made in the same way. The creamy filling is poured into the centre of a cooked pastry case rather than lying under a pie-crust top. Exactly the same ingredients are needed but the instructions are as follows.

Make the seafood mixture as in the above recipe.

To make the vol-au-vent case roll out the puff pastry into a circle about the size of a dessert plate or a large side plate. It should be about the thickness of two large coins one on top of the other. With a very sharp knife cut out an even round, making sure that all the edges are cleanly cut. With the blade of the knife held parallel to the tabletop knock up the edges of the pastry all round, i.e. make little cuts in the side of the pastry piece to encourage the layers to separate once they get into the oven. Now with the tip of the knife mark a second circle inside the round of pastry leaving about 1½ in (4 cm) of border. You should cut through the top layer of pastry but by no means right through to the tabletop or board. This inner circle is to be the lid.

Heat the oven to 230°C/450°F/Gas Mark 8, and put a pan or dish of water in the bottom of it. This is to provide a steamy atmosphere which will encourage the pastry to rise well. Once the oven is hot put the vol-au-vent round on a baking tray and bake it for twenty minutes or so, or until well risen and very brown. Take it out and, using a serrated knife, carefully cut and lift away the middle section of pastry. Keep this for the lid. Using a spoon, scrape out any uncooked pastry from the inside of the vol-au-vent. Put the pastry case back in the oven to dry out the middle.

Heat the filling in a saucepan, double boiler or in the bottom of the oven, without boiling it. Just before serving reheat the pastry case if it has been allowed to get cold, put it on a warmed serving platter and pour in the hot filling. Replace the pastry lid and serve at once.

Grilled sea bass with fennel

One of the best ways of cooking a whole sea bass is to grill it in the conventional manner, that is, under a medium heat, brushed with butter and sprinkled with a little lemon juice. When the fish is cooked put some sticks of dried fennel in a roasting tin and fix the fish, lain on a trivet or grill rack, over the fennel sticks, light the fennel and allow the burning herb to perfume the fish and char the skin slightly. Work chopped fresh fennel, if you have it, into salted butter and serve the fish with slices of this on each portion.

Puff pastry

Perfectly adequate frozen puff pastry can be bought almost anywhere nowadays. Of course if you are a really keen cook, and have the time to go at it in a leisurely and relaxed way, rich, crisp and buttery home-made puff pastry is unbeatable.

½ lb (225 g) plain flour
1 oz (30 g) lard
5 oz (140 g) butter
¼ pint (150 ml) icy water
Pinch salt

Sift the flour with the salt. Cut the lard into tiny dice, then rub it into the flour, using floured fingertips. Add the cold water and mix with a knife to a soft dough. Turn the dough onto the tabletop and knead until smooth. Wrap in plastic film and leave in the refrigerator for twenty minutes.

Roll the dough into a rectangle about 5 in by 10 in (13 cm by 25 cm). Tap the butter lightly with a floured rolling pin to get it into a flattened block about 3 in (8 cm) square. Put it on the pastry and fold both ends over to enclose it. Press the sides together to prevent the parcel opening up.

Now tap the pastry parcel with the floured pin to flatten it further. Then roll out until the pastry is three times as long as it is wide. Fold it in three, first folding the end closest to you over, then bringing the top third down. Give it a ninety degree anti-clockwise turn so that the folded, closed edge is on your left. It should now look rather like a closed book with the loose flap of pastry on your right. Again press the edges firmly with the rolling pin. Then roll out again to form a rectangle as before.

Now the pastry has had two 'turns' (rolls and folds). The rolling and folding must be repeated twice more, the pastry again rested, and then given two more 'turns'. This makes a total of six. Keep wrapped and cool until needed.

Crab with brandy and cream sauce

The shell, neatly trimmed with pliers, can be kept and used as a serving dish. Or a good crab bisque could be made using the crushed remains (recipe p. 47).

Do not be tempted to freeze the mixture – it needs to be very fresh. The left-over brown part is good beaten up with butter and chopped chives to make a crab and chive paste.

¾ lb (340 g) freshly boiled crab

For the sauce:
1 oz (30 g) butter
2 oz (55 g) chopped onions or shallots
1 tablespoon flour
8 fluid oz (235 ml) fish stock or liquid in which the crab was cooked
¼ pint (150 ml) double cream
2 tablespoons brandy
Salt, pepper
Pinch of chilli powder

To serve:
Boiled rice
Fleurons (recipe below)

Serves 4

If your fishmonger will take the flesh from the crab, so much the better. If not, or if you have boiled it yourself, proceed like this. Remove the legs and the claws. Separate every part at the joints. Gently crack the larger ones open. The flesh can be pushed from the smaller ones with a skewer without cracking. Small splinters of shell are a plague and can easily hurt the mouth or teeth of the diner so be very careful to remove them all. Remove the under-shell (crack round the edge of the underside with something heavy). Remove as much flesh as you can from the body and from every crevice, keeping the brownish flesh and soft matter separate from the white firm flesh.

Heat the butter in a small pan and gently fry the onions or shallots in it until they are soft. Add the flour, stir until well mixed, then add the stock, the cream and the brandy. Stir until boiling, then simmer gently. Adjust the seasoning, including the chilli powder as well as salt and pepper. Place the crab meat in a serving-dish, cover with the sauce, and arrange the pastry *fleurons* all round. Serve with pilau rice.

Fleurons

¼ lb (110 g) puff pastry
Beaten egg

Roll the pastry out to the thickness of a large coin. Using a fluted cutter stamp out small crescents. Brush with egg and bake in a hot oven (230°C/450°F/Gas Mark 8) for twelve minutes or until risen and brown.

Mushroom and fish kebab with anchovy butter

Firm-fleshed fish like turbot are best for this, but any good white fish will do.

1 lb (450 g) white fish fillet, skinned
½ lb (225 g) button mushrooms
Black pepper
About 3 oz (85 g) butter
2 anchovy fillets, finely chopped
Anchovy essence
Chopped parsley
Lemon juice

Serves 4

Skewer the mushrooms with the fish (cut into neat cubes) on four metal skewers. Brush all over with melted butter and sprinkle with black pepper. Grill steadily for ten minutes or so, turning frequently. When the fish has begun to brown, and feels firm to the touch, remove the kebabs and put them on a serving-dish. In a frying pan or the bottom of the grill tray, melt about 2 oz (55 g) butter and stir into it a good dessertspoon of anchovy essence. Add the chopped anchovy fillet, the parsley and the lemon juice. Heat together until sizzling, then pour over the kebabs and serve at once.

Grilled mackerel with mustard sauce

The sauce in this recipe is one of those quick and easy modern sauces, using nothing more than a bowl and a spoon. If the mackerel is fresh the dish cannot be bettered.

4 small mackerel, or 2 large ones split in half with the bones removed
Butter for grilling

For the sauce:
1 tablespoon pale French mustard
1 carton soured cream
1 carton yogurt
Lemon juice
Freshly ground black pepper, salt

Grill the mackerel on both sides until it feels firm to the touch and a skewer will glide easily into the flesh. Dish the fish neatly on a serving-dish and squeeze over a little lemon juice. Season lightly with salt and grind black pepper fairly liberally on top. Mix together the soured cream, yogurt and mustard, and season it well with salt, pepper and if necessary a little more lemon juice. Hand a bowl of this sauce separately.

Serves 4

Poultry
and
Game

Leith's duckling

I must apologize to readers who have seen this recipe elsewhere, but I must include it because it is the most popular dish we sell in our restaurant and it is simple to do and, to my mind, one of the best ways of roasting duck.

PL

1 duckling 5–6 lb (2¼–2¾ kg) (which should have a soft, pliable backbone, a dry soft skin – not slimy – and be as plump as possible)

For the sauce:
1 oz (30 g) granulated sugar
1 tablespoon vinegar
1 celery stick, finely chopped
Juice and grated rind of an orange
1 small onion, finely chopped
¼ pint (150 ml) stock
1 dessertspoon brandy
½ oz (15 g) butter
1½ oz (45 g) flaked almonds
Salt, pepper

Serves 2–3

Set the oven to 200°C/400°F/Gas Mark 6. Prick the bird all over, dust it with salt, and put it in the oven to roast for one hour. It needs no fat, but it is a good idea to lay it legs up for the first half hour and turn it right side up for the next half hour. Joint the bird and put the pieces into a clean roasting-pan, skin side up.

Put the sugar and vinegar in a heavy saucepan. Dissolve the sugar over gentle heat until it caramelizes: it will go dark brown and bubbly, with large slow bubbles. Pour on the stock: it will hiss and splutter alarmingly so take care. Stir until the caramel lumps disappear. Add the orange rind and juice and the brandy. Pour over the duck.

Return to the oven and continue cooking until the joints are cooked through (another twenty minutes or so). Do *not* baste. Remove the duck joints onto an ovenproof plate and keep warm. (If the skin is not truly crisp the duck can be returned to the oven for ten minutes like this without the sauce.)

Fry the flaked almonds in the butter until golden brown. Scatter over the duck. Skim the sauce to remove any fat, and strain it into a saucepan. Add the finely chopped celery and onion, and boil until the celery is just beginning to soften but is still a little crunchy (about five minutes). Taste the sauce and add salt and pepper. You should have a thin, fairly clear liquid with plenty of chopped celery and onion in it. Serve the sauce separately, or poured round, not over, the duck.

Poultry

Grilled spicy spring chicken and oriental rice

For the rice:
½ lb (225 g) long-grain or
   Patna rice
1 medium onion, finely
   chopped
1 clove garlic, crushed
1 tablespoon oil
1 tablespoon butter
12 fluid oz (345 ml) well-
   flavoured chicken stock
Pinch turmeric
2 teaspoons sultanas
Salt, freshly ground black
   pepper

For the chicken:
2 double-portion spring
   chickens
½ teaspoon turmeric
¼ teaspoon paprika
½ teaspoon sugar
Juice of ½ lemon
2 teaspoons butter
½ teaspoon made mustard
Salt, freshly ground black
   pepper

Serves 4

Wash the rice well and drain it. Heat the oil and the butter in a large frying pan and gently fry the onion for four or five minutes or until soft and just beginning to colour. Add the garlic and cook for a further half a minute. Add the turmeric, stir well and add the rice. Pour in the chicken stock, season with salt and black pepper and cover the pan. Simmer for fifteen or twenty minutes or until the liquid has been absorbed by the rice and the rice is soft but not mushy. If the pan is in danger of becoming dry add a little water. The rice may take as much as twenty-five minutes. Stir in the sultanas.

Cut each spring chicken in half through the breast and backbone. Clean the inside carefully and trim off any untidy pieces of skin or fat. Lay the chicken, skin side down, in a grill tray. Mix all the remaining ingredients together and use this mixture to coat lightly the upper side of the chicken. Grill under fierce heat until the surface is brown, then lower the heat slightly and continue grilling for four or five minutes or until the colour is very dark. Turn over and brush the skin with the spicy mixture in the grill tray. Grill again until bubbling and brown. Lower the heat until the chicken is tender right through. Serve immediately with the rice.

Casseroled chicken with tomatoes, eggplant and fried onion rings (Arlesienne)

This is a good strong chicken casserole with the highly satisfactory contrast of crisply fried onion rings and aubergine on top. The casserole can be made in advance and kept refrigerated for a day or two, but the eggplant and onion rings must be cooked *à la minute*. Don't be tempted to freeze the chicken casserole; the flesh is liable to become shreddy and dry.

For the casserole:
3½ lb (1.5 kg) chicken, cut in 8 pieces
Oil for frying
Seasoned flour
1 lb (450 g) tinned tomatoes, chopped
1 tablespoon tomato purée
1 medium onion, chopped
1 clove garlic, crushed
Sprig thyme, bay leaf, small bunch parsley, tied together with string
8 fluid oz (235 ml) dry white wine
Salt, freshly ground black pepper

For the garnish:
1 large eggplant (aubergine)
1 large Spanish onion
Fat for deep frying
Milk
Seasoned flour

Serves 4

Follow the method for chicken casserole with tarragon and tomato, omitting the tarragon (p. 104).

For the garnish heat the oil in a deep fryer. Slice the eggplant. Slice the large onion across into rings. Separate all the rings. Keeping onions and eggplant separate, dip them in milk, then shake off the excess milk and dip them in the seasoned flour. Move or shake the pieces around until well coated with flour. Shake off all the excess flour and immediately lower them, a few at a time, into the hot oil. Fry until golden. Remove onto absorbent kitchen paper. Repeat the process until all the onions and the slices of eggplant are done.

Arrange the rings and the slices on and around the hot chicken in a serving-dish. Serve at once, while the onions and eggplant are crisp.

Chicken with Sylvaner cream sauce

Chicken cooked in white wine is very fine. Classically this dish is cooked with German Sylvaner. So, if possible, get a really fruity, flowery, fragrant white wine of the German type. A Yugoslav Riesling would be good, but it should not be too sweet a one. Freezes well, if the pieces are coated with sauce – but the grapes, yolks and cream should not be added until the dish has been reheated.

3½ lb (1.5 kg) chicken
½ pint (290 ml) dry hock
    or similar white wine
½ pint (290 ml) chicken
    stock
Large bunch parsley,
    washed
2 shallots, chopped
1 tablespoon butter
1 level dessertspoon
    flour
¼ pint (150 ml) single
    cream
1 egg yolk
Small bunch sweet white
    grapes, halved, peeled
    and seeded
Salt, pepper

Melt the butter in a saucepan and brown the whole chicken all over. Keep the lid on while you do this, so that the chicken browns and cooks through at the same time. Be careful it doesn't burn. Turn it to brown all sides. After about twenty-five minutes it should be well browned and half cooked. Take it out and joint it. Put the chopped shallots in the pan and cook slowly until soft. Put back the chicken, and add the wine, stock and parsley. Cover and cook until the chicken is tender. Lift out the chicken pieces onto a serving dish and scatter the grapes on top. Cover. Strain the liquid.

Boil the liquid rapidly until there is only ½ pint (290 ml) left. Skim the fat off into a teacup. Mix a dessertspoon of it with the flour and stir it back into the hot liquid. Stir until boiling. Mix the egg yolk and cream together in a bowl. Taste the sauce, adding salt and pepper if necessary. Strain it onto the yolk and cream. Mix well. Pour over the chicken. Reheat without boiling, adding salt and pepper if necessary.

Serves 4

Chicken casseroled in claret

This is one of the many versions of coq au vin. Originally coq au vin was made with a cockerel and the blood was used to thicken the sauce

Put the joints of chicken into a bowl and pour the red wine over them. Add the crushed garlic and the bouquet garni and leave over-night to marinate.

Next day take the chicken pieces out and dry them well on absorbent paper. Keep the

rather as in jugged hare. But live cockerels are hard to find and I doubt if we'd care to find one anyway. The wine used for a coq au vin really makes a difference. Vinegary wine which is undrinkable will produce an absolutely uneatable stew. Once upon a time you could get Coq au Chambertin in Burgundy *auberges* but nobody, not even the gastronomic French, would today use Chambertin to cook with. This version uses inexpensive claret. If there is time to marinate the chicken in the wine before cooking so much the better. Freezes well.

3½ lb (1.5 kg) roasting chicken, jointed into eight pieces
A little flour
About 2 oz (55 g) butter
4 or 5 rashers rindless streaky bacon, diced
Cupful small button mushrooms
Cupful small button onions
½ pint (290 ml) claret
½ pint (290 ml) strong chicken stock
1 clove garlic, crushed
Bouquet garni: bay leaf, sprig of thyme, few sprigs of parsley, tied together with string
Salt, freshly ground black pepper
3 tablespoons brandy
2 slices white bread without crusts
Oil for frying
Chopped parsley (optional)

wine. Heat half the butter in a shallow wide sauté pan and in it fry first the bacon, then the button onions until evenly browned and finally the button mushrooms. Fry fairly fast so that the juice from the mushrooms does not run out. Lift bacon, onions and mushrooms out with a perforated spoon and set aside.

Now dust each piece of chicken in flour, shaking off any excess. Melt a little more butter in the pan and fry the chicken joints on both sides until well browned. Keep the heat fairly high so that they fry rather than stew. Once well browned put back the bacon, onions and mushrooms and pour in the brandy. Set alight, standing back out of the way of the flames. When the flames have died down pour in the wine with the bouquet garni and the stock. Add salt and freshly ground black pepper. Cover the sauté pan and put it in a moderate oven (180°C/350°F/Gas Mark 4) for an hour.

Check to see if the chicken is cooked (a skewer should slide easily into the thick part of the thigh joint). If it is done remove the casserole and skim off any fat. Lift the joints of chicken and the onions and mushrooms out onto a serving-dish. If the sauce is on the thin side boil it rapidly until reduced to a syrupy consistency. Pour over the chicken pieces and keep covered.

For the garnish, pour ¼ in (¾ cm) of oil into a pan and heat up. Cut the two slices of bread into small cubes and fry them in the hot fat, turning them constantly so that they brown evenly. Drain them on absorbent paper. Just before serving scatter the fried croûtons and the parsley all over the casseroled chicken.

Serves 4–6

Grilled baby chicken with mustard

4 one-portion poussins or 2 double-portion spring chickens
2 tablespoons mild, pale French mustard
2 tablespoons double cream
½ teaspoon sugar
Salt, pepper
2 tablespoons fresh white breadcrumbs

To serve:
Watercress

Serves 4

If the chickens are individual-portion size split them open down the back, removing the backbone. Skewer them open and flat by pushing the skewer from one side to the other through the thighs. If they are double-portion chickens split them in half through breast and backbone. Remove the backbone.

Mix the mustard, cream and sugar together and season with salt and pepper. Put the chicken into a grillpan with the skin side down. Spread all over with half the mustard mixture and grill steadily under moderate heat until brown and half cooked. Turn the chicken over, spread the skin side with the rest of the mustard mixture and grill again. The larger double-portion chickens may take as much as twenty minutes, the little ones will be done in about twelve. Just before they are completely cooked sprinkle the breadcrumbs over the skin surface, and using a pastry brush sprinkle with the juices from the grill pan. Put under the grill again to brown and crisp the crumbs. Serve with plenty of watercress.

Spatchcock chicken flamed with Pernod

The preparation of this takes a little time, but the actual cooking is simple. The birds must, however, be cooked at the last minute and eaten as soon as possible.

4 one-portion poussins (baby chickens)
5 tablespoons Pernod
Butter for frying
A little flour
1 medium onion, finely chopped
3 or 4 sprigs tarragon
5 tablespoons single cream
Salt, freshly ground black pepper

Cut each poussin open by splitting down the side of the backbone. Cut away the backbone leaving only the breast and thighs. Open the poussins up and put them inside-down on a board. Flatten them with the palm of your hand and, if possible, stick a metal skewer through them from one leg to the other, securing them open and flat. Heat some butter in a frying pan and fry the chickens, inside-down, until half cooked. Dredge a little flour over the skin of the chicken, then turn over and brown the skin side. When the chickens are cooked through (the whole process will take about twenty minutes) put them all together in the frying pan and pour over the Pernod. Stand back and put a match to the pan. When the flames have died down dish the poussins on a serving-dish.

Chop the tarragon roughly and add it to the juices in the pan. Add the cream and boil up rapidly until a thin sauce is obtained. Pour this sauce into a warm jug and set aside for a minute. Take the same frying pan and melt a teaspoon of butter in it. In this cook the chopped onion until soft and just beginning to turn colour. Add a small sprinkling of flour, just enough to absorb the fat in the pan, and then return the Pernod sauce to it. Boil up, stirring all the time. When bubbling and syrupy in consistency pour over the hot fried poussin and serve at once.

Serves 4

Breast of chicken with prawns, cream and brandy

This is the sort of recipe that I generally disapprove of. You would think that a mixture of chicken and shellfish was less than subtle, and a rich cream and brandy sauce seems to gild the already complicated lily. But I was persuaded against my will to try it and I have to confess that it is quite delicious. Do not be tempted to freeze it.   PL

4 chicken breasts
Butter for frying
¼ lb (110 g) frozen peeled cooked prawns
¼ pint (150 ml) double cream
¼ pint (150 ml) chicken stock
About 1 dessertspoon flour
2 tablespoons brandy
2 shallots, very finely chopped

Melt a tablespoon or so of butter in a wide sauté pan or heavy large frying pan. Cook the shallots in it very gently until they are soft but not at all coloured. Using a perforated spoon lift the shallots out onto a saucer and replace them with the chicken breasts. Turn the heat up and fry the chicken fairly fast on both sides until evenly browned, then fry rather more gently until cooked. Pour in the brandy, stand back a little and set it alight. When the flames die down lift the chicken breasts onto a heated serving-dish, cover and keep warm.

Sprinkle enough flour (about a dessertspoon) into the pan to absorb any fat and stir well, scraping up any sediment stuck to the bottom of the pan. Pour in the stock and stir until boiling. Then add the cream and boil, still stirring, until you have a sauce of the consistency of thin cream. Add the prawns and pour all over the chicken breasts. Serve at once.

Serves 4

Breast of chicken in puff pastry, Madeira sauce

The chicken parcels can be prepared, but not baked, in advance: do not glaze them with milk, but cover well with plastic film or foil and refrigerate until twenty-five minutes before serving. Then brush with milk and bake in a pre-heated oven. They can be kept frozen in the pre-baked state but must be thawed before baking. The sauce can be made in advance, all but the final 2 oz (55 g) of butter, which should be whisked in on reheating.

1 lb (450 g) puff pastry (frozen is fine or see recipe p. 90)
4 boneless chicken breasts
3 oz (85 g) mushrooms, chopped
1 tablespoon chopped onion
About ¼ lb (110 g) butter
5 tablespoons Madeira
¼ pint (150 ml) good chicken stock
¾ oz (20 g) flour
Milk for glazing
Salt, pepper

Serves 4

To make the mushroom *duxelle* melt a tablespoon of the butter in a frying pan and gently fry the chopped onion until golden, then add the chopped mushrooms and one tablespoon of the Madeira. Simmer until all excess moisture has evaporated, leaving a fairly dry mix in the pan.

Season the breasts of chicken and fry them in ½ oz (15 g) of butter for one to two minutes on each side to lightly brown and seal the flesh. Allow to cool.

Roll out the puff pastry to the thickness of a penny, and large enough to cut from it eight pieces of pastry big enough to form tops and bottoms of the chicken parcels. Put the cold chicken breasts on four of the pastry pieces, and divide the *duxelle* between them. Cover with the remaining pastry pieces, wetting the edges with a pastry brush to ensure a good seal. Pierce a small hole on the top of each parcel to release steam while cooking.

Heat the oven to 220°C/425°F/Gas Mark 7.

Place the parcels on a baking sheet. Decorate with shapes cut from the pastry trimmings. Brush all over with milk. Bake for ten minutes, then lower the oven to 190°C/375°F/Gas Mark 5 for a further fifteen minutes. Lift onto a serving-dish.

While the chicken is baking make the sauce. Melt ¾ oz (20 g) of butter in a saucepan. Stir in the flour. Cook for half a minute, then blend in the stock and the remaining Madeira. Stir until boiling. Simmer for ten minutes and then check the seasoning. Whisk in 2 oz (55 g) of soft butter bit by bit. Serve the sauce in a warmed gravy boat.

Deep-fried breast of chicken with ginger and lemon

The very light crisp batter is Chinese in origin and the lemony ginger flavour, though exotic, is quite delicious. It really needs a cook in the kitchen, however, because it is difficult to deep fry food without ending up with one's hair smelling like a chip shop. If you must do it yourself, wear a chef's hat or a shower cap.

4 chicken breasts, skinless
¼ lb (110 g) butter
1 oz (30 g) stem ginger in syrup
1 teaspoon ginger powder
Juice ½ lemon
Oil for frying
A little plain flour

For the batter:

2 oz (55 g) plain flour, sieved
2 oz (55 g) cornflour
1 teaspoon salt
1 oz (30 g) parsley, chopped
8 fluid oz (235 ml) beer
2 egg whites, whipped

For the butter sauce:

½ oz (15 g) butter
1 oz (30 g) onion, chopped
1 oz (30 g) green or red pepper, chopped
2 tablespoons sherry
2 tablespoons double cream
Pinch curry powder
1 teaspoon ground ginger
Salt, pepper

Serves 4

First make the batter. Put the sieved flour, corn-flour, salt and chopped parsley in a mixing bowl. Slowly whisk in the beer until the mixture is light and smooth. Whisk the egg whites until stiff but not dry-looking, and fold in. Allow to rest for two hours.

Now make the sauce. Melt the butter and add the onion and chopped pepper. Cook gently until soft. Add the sherry and simmer for a few minutes. Add the cream, the curry powder, the ground ginger and the salt and pepper. Simmer gently until slightly thick. Check the seasoning, and keep warm.

Lay a breast of chicken flat on the work top. Using a flexible knife, slice it horizontally in its thicker part, but without cutting right through. Then open it out and gently beat it with a mallet or rolling pin to spread it flat. Repeat the process for all the breasts.

Chop the stem ginger and mix with the soft butter. Spoon into four small sausage-like shapes, and place one on each of the flattened breasts. Roll the flesh around the butter, en-suring a tight seal at the joins.

Heat the frying oil until a crumb will sizzle vigorously in it. Dust the chicken with plain flour, then coat with the batter. Lower into the hot frying oil. Fry for eight to ten minutes until golden. Remove and drain on a sheet of absorbent paper. Dish on a hot serving plate and serve with the sauce handed separately.

Note. When eating the chicken pieces cut the pointed tip of the breast before slicing through. This will release the melted butter and prevent it splashing or squirting out when the chicken parcel is cut in half.

Deep-fried breasts of chicken stuffed with spinach and ham

This recipe is a variation of the famous chicken à la mode de Kiev, when the breast of chicken is stuffed with a lump of very cold butter, often flavoured with garlic, parsley or lemon. The present version is more substantial, containing strips of ham and buttery spinach. It can be frozen when prepared for the fryer but not yet cooked. Thaw before frying.

4 whole chicken breasts, skinned and boned
½ lb (225 g) spinach
Salt, pepper
2 thin slices ham, cut into strips
2 oz (55 g) butter
Flour
Beaten egg
Breadcrumbs
Fat for deep frying

Serves 4

Put the chicken breasts between two pieces of polythene or greaseproof paper and, using a mallet or rolling pin, beat them out until they are flat and look like a veal escalope. They should be at least the size of your outspread hand.

Cook the spinach (washed and de-stalked) in rapidly boiling water for half a minute. Drain under cold running water, then squeeze out as much moisture as you can. Chop the spinach, season it with salt and pepper, and butter it well. Put a tablespoon or so of chopped spinach onto each chicken breast and add a lump of cold butter (about a teaspoon for each chicken). Cut the ham into very fine shreds and divide it among the chicken escalopes.

Now roll each chicken breast up like a long parcel, making sure that the breast overlaps so that there are no gaps. Roll the parcels first in flour then in beaten egg and finally in dried breadcrumbs. Put them on a plate, slightly apart, and chill well, or put into the freezer for half an hour. Heat the fat until a crumb will sizzle vigorously in it. Just before serving lower the chicken pieces, all together, into it. Deep fry until evenly brown. This should take about eight minutes. Serve at once.

Chicken casserole with tarragon and tomato

The chicken casserole can be made a day or two in advance and kept refrigerated. Do not freeze, however.

3½ lb (1.5 kg) chicken
Oil for frying
Seasoned flour

Joint the chicken into eight pieces. Season all the chicken pieces with salt and pepper. Roll lightly in seasoned flour. Heat two table-spoons of oil in a frying pan, then fry the chicken on all sides until evenly browned. Lift the pieces into a saucepan. Now fry the chopped onion until soft and just turning colour, then add the tomatoes, the tomato purée, crushed garlic and the stalks (but not the leaves) of the tarragon tied together with

1 lb (450 g) tinned
   tomatoes, chopped
1 tablespoon tomato
   purée
1 medium onion, chopped
1 clove garlic, crushed
Few sprigs tarragon
Sprig thyme, bay leaf,
   small bunch parsley
8 fluid oz (235 ml) dry
   white wine
Salt, freshly ground
   black pepper

the other herbs. Boil the white wine rapidly for five minutes, then add to the saucepan. Simmer gently under a lid for thirty minutes or until the chicken is tender.

Remove the bunch of herbs, check the seasoning, and stir in the chopped tarragon leaves. Add a teaspoon of sugar if the tomatoes are very acid. If the sauce is on the thin side, lift out the chicken with a perforated spoon and boil the sauce fast until syrupy, then return the chicken.

Serves 4

Breast of chicken stuffed with Gruyère and prawns

Another dish on the chicken/prawns/cream and brandy theme. This time the chicken is wrapped round the prawns, and the inclusion of a little Gruyère is surprisingly good.

4 chicken breasts, boned
   and skinned
2 oz (55 g) cooked peeled
   prawns
2 oz (55 g) Gruyère cheese
1 oz (30 g) plain flour
1 oz (30 g) butter
¼ pint (150 ml) double
   cream
3 tablespoons brandy
Salt, pepper
½ teaspoon pale French
   mustard

Lay a breast of chicken flat on the work top. Using a flexible knife, slice it horizontally in its thicker part, but without cutting right through. Then open it out and gently beat it with a mallet or rolling pin to spread it flat. Repeat the process for all the breasts.

Chop the prawns roughly. Dice the Gruyère cheese. Divide the mixture between the chicken pieces. Fold carefully to enclose the filling tightly. Sprinkle lightly with plain flour, then fry gently in foaming-hot butter for six or seven minutes each side. Avoid handling and turning too often. Lift out the chicken parcels and keep them warm, covered, in a serving-dish.

Pour the brandy into the frying pan and set alight to burn off the alcohol. Add the cream. Season with salt and pepper and whisk in the mustard. Reduce by boiling until the sauce is slightly thickened, then check for seasoning. Pour the sauce over the suprêmes, and serve immediately.

Serves 4

Stuffed breast of turkey, port wine sauce

This is a fairly hefty dish, perfect for a cold winter's day or a dinner party where everyone has skipped lunch. The dish can be cooked a day or two in advance and will keep in a refrigerator. Freezing is less satisfactory.

Four 5 oz (140 g) raw
   thin breast of turkey
   slices
6 oz (170 g) raw dark
   turkey meat
About 2½ oz (70 g) butter
2 oz (55 g) carrots, finely
   chopped
1 oz (30 g) onions,
   chopped
2 slices white bread,
   soaked in milk
1 tablespoon chopped
   parsley
1 egg white, lightly beaten
Salt, freshly ground black
   pepper
3 tablespoons double
   cream
Flour
About ¾ pint (425 ml)
   chicken stock
5 tablespoons ruby port

Serves 4

First make the filling. Mince the dark turkey meat twice, the second time mincing the bread with it. Melt ½ oz (15 g) of the butter in a frying pan and gently cook the carrots and onions in it until soft but not coloured. Place the minced meat and bread in a mixing bowl, add the cooked vegetables, the chopped parsley and the white of egg. Season with salt and pepper and mix thoroughly. Now slowly beat in the double cream until a soft paste is obtained.

Put each turkey slice between pieces of foil or greaseproof paper and on the tabletop beat with a mallet or rolling pin to flatten and enlarge them. Then divide the stuffing between them and roll them up. Tie them up loosely with fine string. Roll lightly in plain flour. Heat a tablespoon of butter in the frying pan and fry all over until evenly brown. Cover with the stock and port, and simmer gently for forty-five to fifty minutes, or until very tender. Lift the turkey rolls out of the liquid, discard the strings and put into a serving-dish. Keep covered while finishing the sauce. Boil the liquid until a syrupy consistency, then whisk in the remaining 1 oz (30 g) of butter, and strain over the turkey.

Quail

Quails with grapes and pine nuts

This recipe assumes that the diners are hungry enough to eat two quails each. For a lighter or less expensive dinner one fat quail each would do, served perhaps on a croûton of fried bread to bump it up a bit.

8 quail
4 fatty rashers bacon, rindless
1 shallot, finely chopped
Salt, freshly ground black pepper
Bouquet garni: bay leaf, few sprigs parsley, sprig thyme, tied together with string
¼ lb (110 g) small seedless green grapes, or failing them larger green grapes, seeded and peeled
3 fluid oz (85 ml) white wine
3 fluid oz (85 ml) chicken stock (or water with ½ stock cube)
2 teaspoons flour
2 tablespoons double cream

To serve:
Small bunch watercress
2 oz (55 g) pine nuts

Set the oven to 190°C/375°F/Gas Mark 5. Wipe the quails inside and out with a clean damp cloth. Put a small piece of bacon on the top of each quail, covering the breast as far as possible. Put the quails in a roasting-pan and give them a few twists of the black pepper-mill. Pour in the stock and wine and add the chopped shallot, the bouquet garni and the salt and pepper. Cook the quails uncovered in the oven for fifteen minutes and then remove the pieces of bacon. Return to the oven for a further fifteen minutes or until the breasts of the birds are pale gold and a skewer will glide easily through the thigh. Dish the quails on a serving-dish and cover them with a piece of foil. Keep them warm.

Remove the bouquet garni from the pan juices and skim off any fat. Mix a little of this fat with the flour to make a smooth paste and then whisk it back into the sauce. Put the roasting-tin directly over the heat. Stir until it boils, then taste and add more salt and pepper if necessary. Strain the sauce into a clean saucepan and add the grapes and cream. Reheat and pour over the quails. Put the pine nuts into a dry frying pan and shake them over moderate heat until evenly and lightly coloured. Just before serving scatter the nuts all over the top of the quails and decorate the dish with a few sprigs of watercress on top.

Serves 4

Quails in pastry

These little parcels of quail look very festive and attractive, and have the advantage of plenty of pre-preparation and little last-minute fiddling. The quails can be wrapped in the pastry, the parcels glazed and decorated and kept in a cool place until the last minute. They then need only be roasted while guests have a pre-dinner drink, or eat their first course. Boning quails is a real fiddle for the inexperienced, so order them ready-boned.

4 fat quails, boned
¾ lb (340 g) puff pastry (frozen is fine or see recipe p. 90)
Butter for frying
2 shallots, finely chopped
2 oz (55 g) chicken or duck livers
¼ lb (110 g) sliced mushrooms
2 tablespoons brandy
Salt, pepper
Beaten egg

For the sauce (optional):
½ pint (290 ml) good stock
3 tablespoons Madeira
¾ oz (20 g) flour
¾ oz (20 g) butter
Salt, pepper

Serves 4

First make the stuffing. Melt a lump of butter in a frying pan and in it fry first the chopped shallot until soft and just beginning to turn colour, then add the chicken livers (with any discoloured parts removed) and fry fairly fast until the livers are brown on the outside but still pink in the middle. Lift out the livers and put in the mushrooms. Shake the pan over a fairly high heat for two or three minutes until the mushrooms are just brown at the edges. Mash the chicken livers roughly with a fork and mix them with the shallots and mushrooms. Season this mixture well with salt and pepper and add the brandy. Spoon into the cavity in the quails. Do not worry if the quails are not properly filled. Brush them lightly with butter and grill them under a fierce heat on all sides until browned but not completely cooked – about five or six minutes. Allow them to get cold.

Roll out the pastry into a very large thin sheet. Cut it into four, each piece being large enough to envelop a quail completely. Put the quails on the pastry and wrap up, using beaten egg to stick the edges together tightly. Put the pastry parcels on a baking sheet with the joins underneath and the smooth sides up. Brush all over with beaten egg and use any pastry trimmings to make leaves or other decorations for the top. Brush these with egg too.

Heat the oven to 230°C/450°F/Gas Mark 8. Twenty minutes before serving put the quails near the top of the oven. After ten minutes the pastry will be puffed up and beginning to brown and the quails can now be moved to the bottom of the oven (or if the oven is even-tempered all over it can be turned down to 200°C/400°F/Gas Mark 6).

The quails may be served with a thin sauce if desired. To make this boil the ½ pint (290 ml) of stock and 3 tablespoons Madeira together until reduced to about 8 fluid oz (235 ml). Thicken this liquid with ¾ oz (20 g) flour and ¾ oz (20 g) butter, beaten together to a smooth paste and then whisked into the boiling liquid bit by bit. Taste and add salt and pepper if necessary.

Quail with brandy cream sauce

Many people complain that quail are a fiddle to eat. This is not true if fingers are allowed. So provide finger bowls and large linen napkins.

4 large quail
4 slices white bread
  without the crusts
Butter for frying
2 oz (55 g) chicken or
  duck livers
$\frac{1}{4}$ pint (150 ml) cream
1 shallot, finely chopped
5 tablespoons brandy
A little butter
Salt, freshly ground
  black pepper

Serves 4

Spread the quail breasts with butter and put them into a buttered metal roasting-tin. Heat the oven to 220°C/425°F/Gas Mark 7 and roast the quail for twenty minutes or until slightly brown and cooked through. Remove the birds and keep them warm.

While the quail is in the oven fry the slices of bread in butter until brown and crisp on both sides. Put on a plate and keep warm, uncovered. Using the same frying pan and a little more butter if necessary, gently cook the chopped shallot until soft and just beginning to turn brown. Trim any discoloured parts from the chicken livers, then add them to the frying pan. Cook fairly fast, turning them once, until brown and firm to the touch but still slightly pink in the middle. Pour in the brandy and set it alight.

Once the flames have died down mash the chicken livers with a fork until you have a soft paste. Remove from the heat and add salt and plenty of black pepper. Spread this mixture on the fried bread. Put any juices that have run from the quails during roasting into the frying pan and add the cream. Using a fish slice or wooden spoon scrape up the bottom of the pan and mix well. Boil up the cream and allow it to bubble until fairly thick. Pour over the quail and serve immediately.

Game

Pheasant with pickled cabbage and sausages

Only the sausages can be prepared at all in advance. But the cooking and serving are simple and do not require much of the cook's time.

2 young pheasants
Butter
1 glass sweet red wine or ruby port
8 or 10 juniper berries, crushed
6 rashers streaky bacon
1 lb (450 g) tin sauerkraut
8 cocktail-size pork sausages
½ pint (290 ml) stock
1 level dessertspoon flour
Salt, freshly ground black pepper

Serves 5–6

Roast the pheasant as described for grouse (p. 114), putting the crushed juniper berries inside the bird in place of the cranberries, and using the streaky bacon to cover the breasts. They will take forty minutes for rare birds and fifty-five for well done. When they are cooked remove them from the pan and keep warm.

While the pheasant is roasting fry the sausages in a little butter to brown them evenly all over. Heat up the sauerkraut, drain it well and spread it on a warm, flat serving-dish. Brush it with butter and grind black pepper all over it. Shake the juniper berries out of the pheasant into the roasting tin and put the pheasant on top of the cabbage. Surround with the fried sausages and keep warm while you make the sauce.

Put the pan with the roasting juices and the juniper berries over the heat and whisk in the dessertspoon of flour. Add the stock and bring to the boil, stirring steadily. Simmer for two or three minutes and season with salt and pepper. Hand the sauce round separately or pour it over the pheasant and sausages.

Roast pheasant with red cabbage

The red cabbage can be cooked well in advance. It keeps well for a few days in the refrigerator or longer in the freezer. Proceed as for roast pheasant above, omitting the sauerkraut and sausages, and serve instead with the red cabbage stewed as described below.

Red cabbage

Red cabbage takes a long time to cook, but requires little effort on the part of the cook. It freezes well.

2 lb (900 g) red cabbage, finely shredded
2 medium onions, finely sliced
1 heaped dessertspoon brown sugar
1 tablespoon sultanas
3 dessert apples, cored and chopped but not peeled
Pinch dried mustard
1 wine glass vinegar
1 wine glass water
Salt, black pepper

Serves 6

Put all the ingredients into a heavy-bottomed saucepan that has a well-fitting lid. Make sure the mixture is well seasoned with plenty of black pepper, but not too much salt. Set over a very gentle heat or in a coolish oven and stew gently, giving the pan a shake every now and again to prevent the cabbage sticking to the bottom. After two to three hours the cabbage should be reduced to a soft, slightly thickish mixture with just enough moisture remaining to coat the leaves nicely. If there remains too much liquid remove the lid and boil rapidly, stirring occasionally until the right consistency is obtained.

Bread sauce

4 cloves
Few slices onion
Good pinch ground nutmeg
1 bay leaf
½ pint (290 ml) milk
2 slices white bread without the crusts
2 oz (55 g) butter
Salt, white pepper

Put the cloves, onion, nutmeg, bay leaf and milk into a saucepan and bring slowly to the boil. Once it is boiled set aside to infuse for ten minutes or so. Strain the still warm milk onto the bread. Break up with a fork and mix well. Return the mixture to the saucepan and stir while bringing to the boil. Once hot, beat in the butter and flavour with salt and pepper.

If the sauce is allowed to stand it may become stodgy. Add a little top of the milk, cream, or milk and beat well. Bread sauce should have a thick but creamy consistency – more a cream than a paste.

Pheasant casserole with chestnuts

Will keep well for a week in the fridge. Also freezes. well. Thaw before reheating, and resist any temptation to stir, which would break the pheasant flesh into shreds.

2 young pheasants
Butter for frying
12 button onions, peeled
12 small Paris mushrooms
12 fresh chestnuts
$\frac{1}{2}$ pint (290 ml) red wine
$\frac{1}{2}$ pint (290 ml) chicken stock
2 or 3 rashers rindless streaky bacon, diced
Salt, pepper
Bouquet garni: bay leaf, sprig parsley, sprig thyme, stick celery, tied together with string
2 teaspoons redcurrant jelly
$\frac{3}{4}$ oz (20 g) flour and $\frac{3}{4}$ oz (20 g) butter, mixed together to a paste

Serves 6

Cut the pheasants into four or eight neat pieces.

Melt 1 oz (30 g) of butter in a frying pan and quickly brown the pieces of pheasant on both sides. Lift them out and put them in a casserole. Next brown the peeled onions in the same way, adding more butter if necessary. Then fry the button mushrooms for three or four minutes. Put the onions in a casserole with the pheasant but set aside the mushrooms.

Pour a little of the red wine into a frying pan, swish it about and boil up. Pour this mixture, and any sediment from the bottom of the pan, on top of the pheasant in the casserole. Add the rest of the red wine, the chicken stock, the bouquet garni, the pieces of diced bacon, and salt and pepper. Cover the casserole and bring to simmering point. Simmer, either over low heat or in a moderate oven (180°C/350°F/Gas Mark 4) until the pheasant is tender – about forty minutes.

Meanwhile prepare the chestnuts. Make a large slit in the tough skin of each chestnut from the point to the rounded end. Put them in a pan, cover them with hot water and bring them to the boil as quickly as possible. Take the pan from the heat and, using rubber gloves so that you can handle the chestnuts while they are really hot, lift them out one by one and peel them. Once peeled melt a little more butter in a frying pan and fry the chestnuts in it until well browned.

When the button onions and the pheasant in the casserole are tender take the pot off the heat and strain off all the liquid. Throw away the bunch of herbs and put the solid ingredients into a deep serving-dish. Cover them with a piece of foil and keep warm in a slow oven while you make the sauce.

Put the strained cooking liquid back over the heat and boil rapidly until reduced to about $\frac{2}{3}$ pint (380 ml). Taste and add salt and pepper if necessary. Into this boiling liquid gradually whisk the butter and flour paste, adding small bits at a time. By the time all of it is in you should have a thin, slightly syrupy sauce. Add the mushrooms and the redcurrant jelly, stir until the jelly is melted, and then pour the sauce over the pheasant. Scatter the fried chestnuts on top and serve at once.

Fried crumbs for game and poultry

1 cupful white, slightly
  stale, breadcrumbs
3–4 oz (85–110 g) butter

Heat the butter until foaming and tip in the breadcrumbs. Turn the heat to moderate and, using a fish slice or wooden spoon, keep the crumbs moving all the time they are frying. If the crumbs promptly absorb all the butter add a little more. Keep frying until the crumbs are browned, crisp and very buttery. Bread-crumbs are frequently under-fried so that they are a soggy paste. It is important to keep the crumbs moving, or some of them will burn while others of them are still soft and pastey. Tip the hot crumbs into a warm serving-dish and pass round with a deep spoon or ladle.

Guinea-fowl in cream and Calvados

A luxurious dish for special occasions. It can be prepared well in advance, even the day before. It does freeze but the results are not as good as if the dish is freshly made.

2 young guinea-fowl
About 2 tablespoons flour
About 2 oz (55 g) butter
2 shallots, finely chopped
2 large dessert apples
1 tablespoon Calvados
¼ pint (150 ml) good
  chicken stock
8 fluid oz (235 ml) dry
  cider
Bouquet garni: bay leaf, 2
  or 3 parsley stalks and
  sprig of thyme, tied
  together with string
Salt, freshly ground black
  pepper
4 tablespoons double
  cream

Serves 4–6

Cut each guinea-fowl into four neat joints. Shake them in flour. Heat a tablespoon or so of the butter in a deep wide frying pan or sauté pan and brown the pieces on both sides. When they are well browned lift them out with a perforated spoon and set aside.

Brown the chopped shallot fairly slowly so that they soften as well as colour slightly. Peel the apples and cut into neat segments. Dip these lightly in flour and fry them too, adding more butter if necessary. Lift out the apple pieces, leaving the shallot in the pan. Keep the apple warm. Return the guinea-fowl to the pan and pour in the Calvados. Stand back and set a match to it. When the flames have died down pour in the chicken stock and the cider. Add the bouquet garni, half a teaspoon of salt and four or five twists of the black pepper-mill. Cover the pan and simmer gently until the guinea-fowl is tender – about forty-five minutes.

Once the pieces are tender lift them out and put them on a heated serving dish. Throw away the bouquet garni. Boil the remaining liquid rapidly until reduced to a syrupy consistency. Taste and add more salt and pepper if necessary, then stir in the cream. Pour the sauce all over the guinea-fowl and arrange the apple slices on top.

Roast grouse with cranberries

In autumn I'm certain that my favourite food is grouse, just as in winter it is parsnips, in spring it is sea trout, and in July it is raspberries. I have a distinct prejudice about out-of-season food. Grouse is a dreadful price but it does repay the expense in pure gastronomic pleasure. They may be served either as in the recipe below, with a conventional gravy flavoured with cranberries, or in the traditional way with bread sauce, redcurrant jelly, the juices from the roasting-pan, and with fried buttered breadcrumbs. The method of frying bread-crumbs and making bread sauce is given on pp. 111 and 113.   PL

4 young grouse
Butter
1 glass ruby port or
    strong sweet red wine
Salt, freshly ground
    black pepper
¼ lb (110 g) cranberries,
    fresh, tinned or frozen
4 rashers fatty bacon
4 slices white toast
1 teaspoon flour
⅓ pint (190 ml) stock
Sugar to taste
1 bunch watercress
    (optional)

Serves 4

Set the grouse livers aside. Wipe the grouse inside and out with a clean damp cloth, then put them into a small roasting-tin. Spread them with a little butter and grind pepper fairly generously all over them. Fill the cavities of the grouse with the cranberries and put the bacon over the top of the breast. Pour the wine into the roasting tin and add a quarter of a teaspoon salt to the pan. Heat the oven to 200°C/400°F/Gas Mark 6, and when it is hot put in the bird to roast. Baste once or twice during the cooking, and remove the pieces of bacon from the breasts ten minutes before the end of the cooking time to allow the birds to brown nicely. Remove the birds after thirty or forty minutes depending on whether you want them rare or well done.

While the grouse are cooking fry the livers quickly in butter, then mash them to a paste with a little more butter. Season this with salt and pepper. Cut off the crusts of the pieces of toast and spread with the liver mixture. Put the toast on a heated serving-dish. Tip the cranberries out of the grouse into the roasting tin and lay the grouse on top of the toast. Keep warm. Put the roasting tin with the cranberries in the teaspoon of flour. Add the stock and stir steadily until boiling. Season with salt, pepper and, if sour, a little sugar. Serve the sauce separately. Garnish the grouse with a few sprigs of watercress if liked.

Mr Reynaud's juniper hare

This dish consists of a rich stew made of the legs and neck of the hare, topped with slices from the succulent and pink roast saddle. Ideally the pieces of hare should be marinaded for three or four days in the wine. My grandmother had a lovely earthenware pot for this, but a plastic bucket will do. The stew part of the dish may be cooked the day before or even frozen well in advance and reheated when required.   JBR

4½ lb (2 kg) hare
½ lb (225 g) carrots, peeled
   and sliced
¼ lb (110 g) onions,
   peeled and sliced
1 celery stick, sliced
½ bottle dry white wine
3 fluid oz (85 ml) wine
   vinegar
¼ pint (150 ml) stock or
   water
1 bouquet garni: bay
   leaf, sprig thyme,
   bunch parsley, tied
   together with string
1 teaspoon crushed black
   peppercorns
1 teaspoon salt
1 clove garlic, crushed
2 oz (55 g) juniper berries
2 teaspoons tomato purée
Flour
Oil for frying

Serves 5–6

Have the butcher cut the hare legs and the neck into pieces. Keep the back (saddle) whole but, using a small sharp knife, remove the outer layer of membrane and sinew. Place the pieces of hare, saddle included, in a plastic container and add all the vegetables, the salt, crushed peppercorns and bouquet garni. Cover with the vinegar and the white wine and leave in the fridge or in a cool place for four days. Move the pieces every twenty-four hours to ensure even marinading.

Remove all the pieces of hare and strain the vegetables, reserving the marinade. Pat the hare dry with a cloth. Set aside the saddle. Dust the rest of the pieces with flour. Heat a little oil in a frying pan and brown the floured joints well on all sides. Lift out and fry the vegetables.

Put all the vegetables and fried hare into a large saucepan and cover with the marinade. Add the stock or water, tomato purée, crushed garlic and juniper berries. Bring to the boil, skim off any froth and fat, then simmer until really tender – two-and-a-half to three hours. (A bit of over-cooking will not hurt: on the contrary.) If the sauce is rather thin, lift out the solid ingredients and boil rapidly to reduce to a syrupy consistency, then pour back over the meat. Check the seasoning for salt and pepper. Heat the oven to 220°C/425°F/Gas Mark 7.

Seal the saddle by frying briskly in hot oil in a shallow pan until brown all over. Then roast in the pre-heated oven for only ten minutes. The flesh should still be pink near the bone. Carefully remove the two large fillets of roasted flesh from either side of the backbone, and the two tiny fillets from underneath. Cut them in thin slices. Arrange these pink slices of saddle on top of the stewed hare and serve immediately.

Collops of venison with cherries

This recipe is for a last-minute game steak with a sweet/sour sauce. It is essential to use either fresh cherries or the tinned Morello cherries. The large fat tinned black cherries are too sweet. The dish will not freeze, but does not take more than ten minutes to make.

1½ lb (675 g) fillet venison cut into 8 small neat rounds
About 2 oz (55 g) butter
About 1 teaspoon coarsely ground black pepper
1 tablespoon brandy
4 tablespoons cream
¼ pint (150 ml) strong beef stock
Salt, pepper
1 teaspoon flour
Pinch dry mustard
Salt
¼ lb (110 g) ripe sour cherries (preferably Morello)
1 teaspoon sugar

Serves 4

Sprinkle the steaks on both sides with the coarsely ground pepper, pressing it well into the flesh with the heel of your hand. Heat 1 oz (30 g) of the butter in a heavy frying pan and quickly fry the steaks on both sides. They should be well browned but pink in the middle. Add the stoned cherries and pour in the brandy. Set alight with a match. When the flames die down lift the steaks out onto a heated serving-dish, cover them loosely with foil, and put in a low oven to keep warm while you make the sauce.

Add the pinch of mustard, the sugar and the teaspoon of flour to the cherries in the pan and stir well with a wooden spoon, scraping up any sediment which may be stuck to the bottom of the pan. Pour in the stock and the cream and stir until boiling. Boil rapidly until you have a sauce of creamy consistency. Add salt and pepper to taste and pour over the steaks. Serve at once.

Meats

Lamb

Tarragon lamb steak with white wine and shallot sauce

This recipe is similar to the garlic steak on p. 124; here the predominant flavour is tarragon. The sauce can be made in advance, but the steaks require last-minute cooking.

4 lamb steaks
4 tablespoons oil
5 or 6 sprigs fresh tarragon
1 clove garlic, crushed
1 medium onion, sliced

For the sauce:
1 medium onion or 3
   shallots, very finely
   chopped
3 fluid oz (85 ml) white
   wine
3 fluid oz (85 ml) chicken
   or veal stock
2 tablespoons chopped
   fresh tarragon
½ oz (15 g) flour
1½ oz (45 g) butter
Salt, freshly ground black
   pepper

Serves 4

Marinate the steaks as described in the garlic lamb steak recipe on p. 124, using the oil, tarragon, onion and garlic for the marinade. When ready to cook the steaks make the wine sauce first. Melt ½ oz (15 g) of the butter in a frying pan and cook the chopped shallots gently until soft and just beginning to turn colour. Add the white wine and boil rapidly until left with two tablespoons of liquid. Sprinkle in the flour and whisk to get a smooth paste. Add the veal or chicken stock and stir until smooth. Taste and add salt and pepper as necessary, and a little more stock or water if the sauce is too thick – it should be on the thin side.

Heat the grill, griddle or frying pan until blazing hot and fry the lamb steaks as fast as possible to seal both sides, then lower the heat slightly and cook for four minutes per side or to your satisfaction (if you cannot tell by the texture take a small cut and have a look). When the steaks are done put them on a serving platter and boil up the wine sauce again. Beat the remaining butter (about 1 oz (30 g)) into it bit by bit and add the chopped fresh tarragon. Pour over the steaks and serve at once.

Walnut-crumbed cutlet with paté filling

These cutlets can be served with a thin tomato sauce, which nicely balances the extreme richness of the paté stuffing and the walnut coating. They can be prepared and coated in advance. Keep refrigerated until the final frying, which must be done just before serving.

4 large best end lamb
    cutlets or 8 small ones,
    trimmed of all fat and
    with the bones
    shortened to about 2 in
    (5 cm)
¼ lb (110 g) chicken livers
1 onion, finely chopped
1 tablespoon brandy
Salt, freshly ground
    black pepper
Butter for frying
½ lb (225 g) walnuts,
    ground into rough
    crumbs
Beaten egg
1 tablespoon chopped
    parsley

To serve:
Thin tomato sauce (recipe
    p. 14) (optional)

Serves 4

First make the paté mixture. Melt a tablespoon of butter in a frying pan and cook the chopped onion until soft but not coloured. Trim any discoloured parts from the chicken livers, then fry the livers rapidly in the butter with the onion for three or four minutes until the chicken livers are brown on the outside but still fairly pink inside. Pour in the brandy and set alight. Give a good few twists of the black peppermill and a sprinkling of salt. Mash the chicken livers with a fork so that you have a rough paste in the frying pan. Scrape the mixture out into a bowl and rinse out the pan. Return the pan to the heat and melt another 1 oz (30 g) or so of butter in it.

Put the well-trimmed cutlets into the foaming butter and fry them rapidly on both sides to brown and seal the meat, but not to cook the middle. Put them on a plate to cool. When stone-cold spread the chicken liver mixture all over both sides of each cutlet and dip them into beaten egg, then coat them with the ground walnuts, pressing gently to make sure that the nuts stick to the egg coating. Chill for half an hour or so.

Heat a good 1 oz (30 g) of butter in the frying pan and brown the cutlets on both sides. As walnuts burn very easily care must be taken to prevent this. Once the cutlets are brown lower the heat and cook very gently to finish cooking the inside of the meat. This should take a further eight or ten minutes, depending on the thickness of the cutlets. Sprinkle with chopped parsley and serve.

Moussaka

There are dozens of moussakas, some with and some without the

Sprinkle the aubergine slices with salt on both sides and leave them on a plate for half an hour for some of their juices to run out.

potatoes, the cheese and egg top, or even the tomatoes. But this is a good peasant version, substantial and garlicky. Personally I do not use olive oil – it has too strong a flavour for me, and costs too much. But classically you should. (Moussaka freezes well, but should be thawed before reheating. Omit the potatoes and do not brown the top until reheating.) PL

1½ lb (675 g) lean lamb, minced
2 medium onions, finely chopped
2 cloves garlic, crushed
1 lb (450 g) fresh tomatoes
3 tablespoons white wine
2 tablespoons tomato purée
Salt, freshly ground black pepper
Water
Good pinch ground nutmeg
1 lb (450 g) aubergine, thickly sliced
2 medium-sized cold boiled potatoes, sliced
Oil (preferably olive) for frying

For the topping:
1 oz (30 g) butter
¾ oz (20 g) flour
½ pint (290 ml) milk
2 egg yolks
2 tablespoons cream
3 oz (85 g) grated strong Cheddar cheese
2 tablespoons breadcrumbs

Serves 4

Heat a tablespoon or so of olive oil (or failing that, any other vegetable oil) in a large heavy saucepan and brown first the onion, then the minced lamb. Lift out the fried food to make room for the next lot – do not fry too much at once.

Dip the tomatoes into boiling water for five seconds, skin them and slice them. When all the meat and onions are browned fry the crushed garlic in a little oil in the saucepan, then add the tomatoes and fry them briefly on both sides, adding more oil if necessary. Add the wine to the tomatoes and boil up rapidly, then add two or three good twists with the peppermill, the tomato purée and the nutmeg. Simmer over a gentle heat for a minute or so and then put back the meat and onion. Now simmer very gently, preferably with a lid, until most of the liquid has evaporated and the sauce looks like the mixture for shepherd's pie. Taste the mince to make sure that it is tender.

Sprinkle salt all over the aubergine. Leave for half an hour. Rinse the slices well to remove any excess salt and pat them dry in a clean tea towel. Heat two or three more tablespoons of olive or vegetable oil in a frying pan and fry the slices on both sides fairly slowly until soft right through and well browned. Watch them, because they burn easily. As the slices are fried lift them out onto a plate. When they are done fry the potato slices in the same way getting them lightly browned on both sides. Put the meat mixture in the bottom of a casserole and cover it with a layer of aubergine. Then arrange the potato on the top of that, seasoning well with salt and pepper as you go. Heat the oven to 200°C/400°F/Gas Mark 6.

To make the topping melt the 1 oz (30 g) of butter in a saucepan, stir in the flour and stir for thirty seconds over a moderate heat. Gradually blend in the cold milk and stir until boiling. You should now have a fairly thick sauce. Add the cream, allow to cool slightly, then beat in the two egg yolks and half the cheese. Pour this mixture all over the potato topping and sprinkle with the rest of the cheese and the breadcrumbs. Put the dish into the oven for thirty-five minutes or until the top is brown and bubbling.

Spring lamb noisettes with bacon and kidney

Ideally these noisettes should be grilled over charcoal. The kidney in the middle should remain pink and the bacon on the outside should be crisp, almost charred. The combination is delightful, and will do for the grandest of dinners. Last-minute cooking, however, is essential.

1 rack of lamb (best end) with the bones removed by the butcher
2 lamb's kidneys
6 rashers streaky bacon, rindless
1 teaspoon chopped fresh thyme
A little butter for grilling
Salt, black pepper

To serve:
1 bunch watercress

Serves 4

If the butcher has not skinned the best end do it now. Lift one corner of the skin with a knife and gripping the skin firmly in your fingers (dip them in salt first: it will make it easier to get a grip) peel the skin off. Put the best end, skinned side down, on a board and sprinkle liberally with salt and pepper. Cut each kidney in half lengthwise and remove the 'core'.

Now roll up the best end, enclosing the kidneys, rolling from the thick end towards the thin flap. Secure the roll in place temporarily with a couple of skewers while you wrap rashers of bacon round it so that the whole roll has a stripey appearance. Tie the roll securely with five or six short pieces of string at 1¼-in (3¼-cm) intervals along the roll. This should hold bacon, lamb and kidney in place.

Now cut between the pieces of string so that each slice is a noisette of lamb with a piece of kidney in the middle and a rasher of bacon round the edge. Lay the slices, or noisettes, flat on the tabletop, press thyme into the meat and grind black pepper all over them. Turn over and treat the other side similarly.

Heat the grill until blazing hot. Melt a little butter in the grill tray and use this to brush one side of the lamb noisettes, and also the grill rack. Put the noisettes, buttered side up, under the grill at its fiercest heat. Grill steadily for three minutes, by which time the noisettes should be fairly well browned. Turn over, brush the other side with butter too and repeat the grilling. Ideally the lamb should be barely pink and the kidney slightly more so, but many people do not like too rare a kidney. Grill the noisettes to your satisfaction (well-done ones will take fifteen minutes in all). It may be necessary to turn the heat down slightly to prevent over-browning.

Dish the noisettes with plenty of well-washed fresh watercress and serve with the juices from the grill tray poured over them at the last minute.

Skewered spring lamb, garlic sauce

1½ lb (675 g) lean best
   young lamb (preferably
   from the leg)
Butter
Black pepper

For the sauce:
4 tablespoons good
   mayonnaise
4 cloves garlic, crushed
4 or 5 sprigs tarragon,
   savoury or thyme,
   finely chopped
Salt, pepper

Skewer the meat and season it with pepper but no salt (salt draws the juices from meat and should be added only after grilling). Mix the ingredients for the sauce together. This will give a strong thick Aïoli-like sauce.

Heat the grill to maximum, then grill the lamb, turning frequently and brushing with butter occasionally. It should not be over-cooked but should be faintly pink inside. Serve with plain boiled rice and the garlic sauce.

To serve:
Plain boiled rice

Serves 4

Skewered lamb with kidney and Armenian hash-hash

Hash-hash is nicer than it sounds – a kind of spicy lamb sausage. With a tomato, lettuce and sweet pepper salad these kebabs are very good – light, spicy and interesting. Start the marinade two or three days in advance.

1 lb (450 g) lean lamb,
   boned, skinned and cut
   into eight pieces
¾ lb (340 g) lean lamb,
   minced
4 lamb kidneys
1 medium onion
2 sprigs parsley, chopped
Pinch fresh chopped
   thyme
¼ teaspoon mixed spice
2 slices bread without
   crusts

For the marinade:
8 fluid oz (235 ml) oil
1 medium onion, minced
1 clove garlic, crushed
Fresh thyme
3 bay leaves

Stir together all the ingredients of the marinade in a plastic or china bowl. Cut the kidneys in half, skin them and remove the white core. Put the eight lamb pieces and the kidneys in the marinade. Move them around to ensure even marinading, and put in a refrigerator for two or three days.

On the day of cooking prepare the hash-hash. Dip the bread in the marinade. In a deep mixing bowl break it up with a fork. Remove about 2 oz (55 g) of minced onions from the marinade and add them to the bowl, with the minced lamb, the parsley, thyme, the mixed spice and salt and pepper to taste. Mix thoroughly with a wooden spatula or by hand. Form the mixture into a dozen small balls.

Cut the onion into quarters, then break it into separate leaves. Spear alternate pieces of lamb, kidney, onion leaves and hash-hash balls on long skewers. Set aside. Get the grill or barbecue fire glowing hot and red before grilling the kebabs. Brush them lightly with the oily marinade and grill for eight to ten minutes, turning them to brown all sides. Serve at once.

1 level tablespoon salt
Pepper
2 oz (55 g) tomato purée
2 pinches cayenne pepper

Serves 4

Garlic lamb steak

This recipe is amazingly simple but it is essential that the steaks be marinated for two or three days at least in the refrigerator. If you can get them a week in advance so much the better. Also it is important that young, tender lamb be used. Last-minute cooking is vital.

4 ½-in (1-cm) lamb steaks weighing about 6 oz (170 g) each, preferably cut from the leg
4 tablespoons oil
4 cloves garlic, crushed
2 or 3 sprigs rosemary, bruised
Freshly ground black pepper, salt
1 mild onion, sliced

To serve:
Watercress, Lamb's lettuce or chicory

Serves 4

Put the lamb steaks into a shallow dish and grind black pepper all over them. Spoon the oil over, making sure they are well covered, and sprinkle with the onion and the crushed garlic. Tuck the well-bruised rosemary into the dish and cover it. Put in the refrigerator for three or four days, giving the steaks a turn every now and then to make sure that the oil keeps them well covered and that the flavours are evenly distributed.

When about to serve, heat the grill to maximum or get a griddle or frying pan very hot. With the fingers strip the oil, or most of it, off the lamb steaks and put them flat onto the grill or frying pan. Brown them as rapidly as you can on each side. They should be served pink in the middle and should not take more than four minutes a side to cook even if they are ½ in (1 cm) thick. Season with salt and freshly ground black pepper.

Serve the steaks with watercress or Lamb's lettuce, or perhaps chicory, as a garnish.

Lamb in pastry

Wrapping meat in pastry is a good way of trapping aroma and flavour. In old cookery books the recipes usually demand the discarding of the

First fry the chops. Heat a tablespoon of the butter in a frying pan and brown both sides of each chop as rapidly as possible. You do not want to cook the inside, just get a good seal to the outside. Remove the chops and allow them to cool on a plate.

pastry once the meat is cooked, but it would be a crime to do that – the pastry has absorbed so much of the juices and flavour of the meat it is almost the best part. The pastry parcels may be prepared well in advance, even brushed with egg glaze. They should be covered loosely in plastic wrap and kept refrigerated until it is time to roast them. Do not freeze unless you have to. If you do, wrap the unbaked parcels well. Thaw completely and brush with egg before baking.

4 double best end cutlets (ask the butcher to divide one best end into four small chops, with only one bone for each piece of meat – this will mean removing every other bone)
½ lb (225 g) field mushrooms or flat black mushrooms, finely chopped
2 oz (55 g) butter
1 medium onion, finely chopped
Squeeze lemon juice
Salt, freshly ground black pepper
Few rosemary leaves
1 lb (450 g) puff pastry (frozen is fine, or see recipe p. 90)
Beaten egg
Salt, pepper

To serve (optional):
Tomato sauce (recipe p. 14)

Meanwhile put the chopped onion in the pan with a little more of the butter and cook gently until soft and just beginning to turn colour. Add the chopped mushrooms, turn up the heat and fry rapidly for one minute. Add a squeeze of lemon juice and plenty of salt and black pepper. Allow this mixture to cool.

Roll the pastry out into a large sheet about as thin as a large coin. Cut the pastry into four pieces large enough to envelop the chops easily, albeit with the bone sticking out. Put a chop onto each piece of pastry so that the meat is centred exactly in the middle of the pastry. Add a spoonful of the mushroom mixture and a leaf or two of rosemary. Fold the edges of the pastry over, wrapping the chop up like a parcel and using some of the beaten egg to seal the edges. The cutlet bone will protrude from one corner of the pastry, but that is as it should be.

Turn the cutlet parcels over and put them on a baking sheet. Brush all over with beaten egg and use the pastry trimming to decorate the tops. Brush again with egg.

Heat the oven to 230°C/450°F/Gas Mark 8 and then bake the cutlets for fifteen minutes or until the pastry is risen and brown. Serve with the tomato sauce if liked.

Swedish lamb

2 lb (900 g) lean lamb
meat, preferably from
the leg, cut into 1 in
(2½ cm) cubes
2 or 3 shallots, peeled
and cut in half
1 small carrot, roughly
cut up
Good handful dill leaves
and stalks (or, if
unavailable, 1 level
tablespoon dill seeds)
Bay leaf
½ teaspoon black pepper
¼ teaspoon salt
1¼ pints (720 ml) chicken
stock (or water and a
stock cube)
1 oz (30 g) butter
¾ oz (20 g) flour
Squeeze lemon juice
1 large or 2 small egg
yolks
4 tablespoons cream

Put all ingredients except the last five listed
into a saucepan, cover with a lid and simmer
until the lamb is tender – about an hour if the
water barely moves. With a perforated spoon
lift the pieces of meat out into a serving-dish,
cover with a lid or foil and keep warm. Strain
the liquid into a bowl and skim off any fat.
If it measures less than ¾ pint (425 ml) make up
the quantity with water.

Melt the butter in the rinsed-out saucepan,
stir in the flour and cook for thirty seconds.
Gradually add the ¾ pint (425 ml) hot stock,
whisking out any lumps as the sauce comes
to boiling point. Add a squeeze of lemon, and
more salt and pepper if necessary. Simmer for
two minutes.

Mix the yolk(s) and cream in a small bowl.
Pour on a ladleful of hot sauce, mix well and
tip back into the pan, taking care not to let the
sauce boil as it reheats. Pour over the lamb and
serve at once.

Serves 5–6

Grilled lamb cutlets with spring herbs

8 French trimmed best
end cutlets (that is, with
nearly all the fat
removed and the bone
shortened to about
2 in (5 cm))
Butter
Salt, freshly ground black
pepper
1 tablespoon chopped
fresh herbs (chervil,
parsley, tarragon,
savoury, thyme and
rosemary are all good,
or a mixture of two
of them can be used)
Squeeze lemon

Grind plenty of black pepper all over the meat.
Dot it with butter. Heat the grill until blazing
hot, then grill the chops on both sides until
well done but still faintly pink in the middle –
they should feel fairly soft to the touch. Dish
them on a plate and sprinkle with salt.

Melt a good lump of butter in the grill pan
or a frying pan and add a squeeze of lemon, a
little salt and pepper and the chopped herbs.
Boil up over direct heat, and pour, still sizzling,
over the cutlets. Put a good bunch of watercress in the middle of the dish and serve at
once.

Serves 4

To serve:
Bunch watercress

Rack of lamb with parsley and garlic

Most butchers sell a rack of lamb with six or seven cutlets on it. Make sure you allow three cutlets to a guest. It is generally advisable to buy two racks for four people rather than one and a half. Ask the butcher to skin the best ends, trim almost all the fat from the rack and shorten the bones so that they do not protrude beyond the meat more than 1 in (2½ cm). The dish is a simple roast, which must be eaten promptly after cooking. Reheating tends to give a dull, rather fatty flavour.

Heat the oven to 220°C/425°F/Gas Mark 7. Mix together the parsley, garlic, butter, salt and pepper and spread this mixture all over the racks of lamb especially on the rounded sides. Put the racks in a roasting-tin and roast, basting once or twice, for forty minutes or until the top is browned and the meat still faintly pink inside. Serve with the buttery juices poured over the lamb, and with a little extra fresh chopped parsley scattered on top to heighten the colour.

2 small best ends lamb
2 tablespoons butter
Good handful parsley,
    finely chopped
2 cloves garlic, crushed
Salt, freshly ground
    black pepper

Serves 4–5

Rack of lamb with mustard and herbs

This recipe is similar to the previous one and the same remarks apply about choosing and butchering the lamb.

2 small best ends lamb
3 tablespoons pale French
    mustard, or 1 table-
    spoon English mustard
1 tablespoon fresh
    chopped tarragon
2 tablespoons fresh
    chopped parsley
1 tablespoon butter,
    melted
2 tablespoons fresh white
    breadcrumbs
Salt, pepper

Mix together the tarragon, parsley and mustard, and season it well with salt and pepper. Spread this mixture over the lamb, especially on the rounded sides. Put the meat into a roasting-tin and press the breadcrumbs all over the top. Sprinkle liberally with the butter. Heat the oven to 220°C/425°F/Gas Mark 7 and when hot roast the lamb for forty minutes or until brown on top and faintly pink inside.

Serves 4–5

Veal

Veal in mild curry sauce with fresh pineapple

This quite delicious creamy veal dish is decidedly rich. It freezes excellently, but this should be done without the pineapple, which can be added just before serving. Thaw before reheating.

1½ lb (675 g) pie veal, carefully trimmed of all sinew
1 pint (570 ml) water
1 chicken stock cube
1 bay leaf

For the sauce:
2 tablespoons oil
1 medium onion, finely chopped
1 tablespoon mild curry paste
1 glass white wine
1 oz (30 g) flour
Salt, pepper
1 slice fresh pineapple (about 2 oz (55 g))
4 tablespoons double cream

Serves 3–4

Cut the pie veal into small pieces and put it in a saucepan. Cover with the water, add the stock cube and the bay leaf. Bring slowly to boiling point, skimming off any scum as it rises. Once it is scum-free set a lid on it and allow to simmer for thirty to forty minutes or until the veal is very tender. Set aside.

Heat the oil in a saucepan and fry the chopped onion until soft and just beginning to colour. Now add the curry paste and cook for a further minute. Add the flour and stir over the heat for thirty seconds or so. Pour in the white wine, stir well and then add ½ pint (290 ml) of the stock in which the veal was cooked. Stir steadily until the sauce boils. Allow to simmer for twenty minutes. If the sauce becomes too thick more stock may be added but if at the end of the simmering time it is still on the thin side boil it rapidly until you have a sauce of creamy consistency. Taste and add salt and pepper as needed. Chop the fresh pineapple and add to the sauce with the cream. Reheat without boiling.

Reheat the veal in its remaining stock, then, with a perforated spoon, lift the pieces of meat into a serving-dish. Pour the sauce over the meat, and serve at once.

Veal escalope, mushroom and ham filling, cream sauce

The mushroom *duxelle* may be made well in advance but the frying of the veal should be done pretty much at the last minute.

4 5-oz (140-g) flattened
   veal escalopes
2 oz (55 g) onions or
   shallots, chopped
1 oz (30 g) chicken livers,
   cleaned and chopped
3 oz (85 g) mushrooms,
   chopped
2 oz (55 g) ham, finely
   chopped
½ teaspoon aniseed
   powder
1 teaspoon chopped
   parsley
Little flour
2 oz (55 g) butter
¼ pint (150 ml) double
   cream
Salt, pepper
Dash Pernod

First prepare the filling (or *duxelle*). Melt 1 oz (30 g) of the butter in a pan and gently cook the chopped shallots or onions until soft. Add the mushrooms, livers, ham and the pinch of aniseed powder. Season with salt and pepper. Stir well and allow any liquid to evaporate. Add the chopped parsley.

Lay the veal escalopes flat on a working top, season carefully on both sides. Place an equal amount of *duxelle* on each. Fold up to enclose the filling, trying to give the same shape to each portion. Dip in flour. Heat the rest of the butter and fry the veal parcels until lightly coloured all over. When the veal is tender and cooked, dish on a warm platter. Pour the cream into the pan, scraping up any stuck sediment with a fish slice or wooden spoon. Season with salt and pepper, and add a dash of Pernod. Simmer until reduced to a thickish sauce, then pour over the escalopes and serve.

Serves 4

Collops of veal with Gruyère and tomato

Buttered French beans or small noodles with tomato sauce are good with this straightforward but delicious dish.

4 6-oz (170-g) veal
   escalopes, well flattened
Little flour
¼ lb (110 g) thin slices
   Gruyère cheese
4 small tomatoes, peeled
2 oz (55 g) butter
Salt, freshly ground
   pepper

Cut each escalope into three or four pieces. Season and flour these 'scallopini', then lightly brown them in sizzling butter. Remove from the pan to a serving-dish.

Slice each tomato in four. Lay a thin slice of Gruyère on each piece of veal, then a slice of peeled tomato. Place the dish under the grill or in a blazing hot oven until the cheese softens. Remove and give them a few twists of the peppermill. Heat the rest of the butter in the frying pan until bubbly. Pour all over the veal and serve at once.

Serves 4

Veal kidney with mushroom and tomato

This dish demands à la minute cooking. If it has to be done in advance the kidneys must be slowly cooked in the sauce for forty minutes or so, to tenderize and 'stew' them. This gives a good but very different dish. The recipe below requires speedy serving, while the kidneys are still tender and pink inside. If left standing for long they will toughen, and will need the further stewing to get them soft again.

1 lb (450 g) veal kidney
About 2 oz (55 g) butter
1 medium onion, finely sliced
½ lb (225 g) best white button mushrooms, quartered
2 tablespoons dry white wine
2 tablespoons tomato purée
2 teaspoons flour
6 fluid oz (175 ml) veal or chicken stock
Salt, pepper

Cut the veal kidneys into slices or pieces roughly the size of the quartered mushrooms. Make sure that all membrane and white parts are removed. Melt 1½ oz (45 g) of the butter in a frying pan and gently soften the onion in it until transparent. Add the mushrooms and cook fairly rapidly until soft – about three minutes. Add the white wine and boil rapidly until the pan is almost without liquid. Stir in the tomato purée and then the flour. Finally blend in the veal or chicken stock and bring to the boil. Season with salt and pepper and set aside.

Just before serving heat a little more butter and rapidly fry the veal kidneys, tossing them and shaking the pan to prevent burning but keeping the heat as high as possible. As soon as the kidneys are done – they should not take more than five minutes – pour on the sauce and check the seasoning, adding salt and pepper if necessary. Serve with plainly boiled rice.

Serves 4

Veal collops on potato and bacon pancake

This dish is simple and delicious but requires the cook's time immediately before serving. The potato mixture may be prepared in advance, but should not be fried until fifteen minutes or so before eating.

First make the potato and bacon pancake. Grate the potatoes. Melt about 1½ oz (45 g) of the butter in a frying pan and gently cook the bacon rashers, chopped into small pieces, until just beginning to turn colour. Add the chopped onion and continue frying until the onion is soft and pale gold. Add the grated potato and using a wooden spoon or spatula flatten the mixture so that a flat pancake is formed. Turn

1 lb (450 g) best Dutch
  veal cut into small
  'scallopini'
1 lb (450 g) large boiled
  potatoes
1 large Spanish onion,
  chopped
4 rashers streaky bacon,
  rindless
About 2 oz (55 g) butter
Salt, pepper
Parsley
Lemon juice
2 tablespoons dry white
  wine

Serves 4

the heat down and fry very gently so that the bottom of the potato mixture browns while the top heats through. To see if the pancake is done lift an edge of it with a spatula or fish slice and peer underneath.

When done put the serving-dish on the table-top and flip the whole pancake over onto it so that the fried side is uppermost (do not worry if it breaks up: simply reshape it). Scrape any stuck bits of the potato out of the frying pan and heat the remaining butter in it. In this quickly fry the veal 'scallopini'. They should be lightly browned on both sides: by this time they will be cooked. Add a little more butter to the pan if it is looking dry, squeeze in the juice of half a very small lemon and add a tablespoon of chopped parsley. Add the two tablespoons of white wine and boil rapidly for thirty seconds. Lift the veal slices out and put them on top of the potato.

Boil the juices up once again, check for seasoning, adding salt if necessary, and pour all over the veal and potato cake.

Peppered veal kidney

A delicious, rather expensive, but dead-easy dish. It requires last-minute cooking, but not much of that – ten minutes in all at the most.   PL

1½ lb (675 g) veal kidney
1½ oz (45 g) butter for
  frying
1 tablespoon green
  peppercorns, tinned or
  frozen
2 tablespoons sherry
4 tablespoons double
  cream
Salt

Serves 4

Cut the veal kidney into very thin slices, discarding any membrane or white parts. If the peppercorns are tinned rinse them under the tap; if frozen they will do as they are, simply thawed.

Heat the butter in a heavy frying pan until foaming. Fry the kidney rapidly so that it browns without releasing any of its juices. A high heat is essential. Keep the pan moving and toss the kidneys in it with a fish slice to prevent them sticking or burning.

When they are brown but still faintly pink inside, lower the heat, pour in the sherry and set it alight. When the flames die down add the peppercorns, shake over the heat for a few seconds, then pour in the cream. Turn up the heat and boil rapidly for a second or two. Add salt to taste. Tip into a warmed serving-dish and serve at once.

Beef and Offal

Rib of beef with Roquefort butter

In restaurants a whole rib of beef is frequently charcoal-grilled and served to two or three people. This is a delicious way of grilling beef, since because the meat is comparatively thick there is little chance of its drying out. Charcoal grills in the home are rare, but the rib can be successfully done in a thick frying pan or, better still, one of those ridged heavy pans which mark the meat with a grill-like lattice. The essential is to get the grill or frying pan blazing hot. The grill tray or rack or the frying pan should be lightly brushed with oil to prevent sticking.

1 or 2 ribs of beef (each rib will serve two or three people)
Freshly ground black pepper, salt

For the Roquefort butter :
3 oz (85 g) butter
3 oz (85 g) Roquefort cheese
Squeeze lemon
Salt, pepper

First make the Roquefort butter by combining the ingredients and putting in a refrigerator to chill well. If liked the butter can be rolled up in a piece of foil or greaseproof paper in a cylinder shape and frozen or well chilled. Round slices can then be cut from the block and served with the steak.

Grind plenty of coarse black pepper all over both surfaces of each piece of meat, pushing them in well with your hand. The steaks should be at room temperature before grilling. Once the grill is blazing hot put the steak under it and quickly grill until well browned. Turn over and repeat for the other side. If the steak is more than 1 in (2½ cm) thick it may be necessary to lower the heat or move the grill pan down a notch so that the outside does not become too hard and burnt. When the meat feels fairly resilient to the pressure of the thumb it will be rare. If it feels tougher it is well done. Blue (very rare) steak feels really soft to the touch. If you are unsure cut a small slit with a sharp knife and have a look.

When the steak is done to your satisfaction sprinkle it with salt and serve it at once with the Roquefort butter. If steak is left to cool and has to be reheated it is unbearably tough. Cut the steak in thin slices at the table.

Fillet of beef in pastry with mushroom stuffing

Ten or fifteen years ago when fillet steak was cheaper than it is now this was the most fashionable of dinner party dishes. Now it costs so much it makes very rare appearances on domestic tables. But it is cheaper than serving whole fillet steaks, and wrapping meat in pastry is a very good way of preserving the flavour and juices of the meat. The whole thing can be prepared well in advance, covered with foil, and kept refrigerated until half an hour or so before serving. Remove the foil and brush with egg before baking. Do not freeze – too much blood will run from the beef on thawing, leaving the pastry soggy and the beef dry.

3 lb (1.35 kg) whole piece of fillet, trimmed of fat and membrane
¾ lb (340 g) puff pastry (frozen is fine or see recipe p. oo)

For the stuffing:
2 medium onions, sliced
½ lb (225 g) mushrooms, chopped
2 oz (55 g) butter
2 oz (55 g) chicken liver paté (recipe p. 37)
Salt, pepper
Beaten egg

Serves 6–8

Fry the sliced onions in the butter. Add the mushrooms and when they are cooked stir in the paté. Season well with salt and pepper, and allow to cool.

Roll out a third of the pastry to a strip about the size of the piece of fillet. Bake it in a hot oven until brown and crisp. Brown the whole fillet in a frying pan or roasting pan (with a little butter or other fat) all over. Allow to cool. Lay the cooked pastry strip on a baking sheet and put the fillet on top. Spoon on the mushroom mixture.

Cover the whole with a top sheet of pastry, and tuck the edges under the pastry base, using a fish slice or palette knife. Brush with egg, decorate lavishly with pastry shapes, and bake at 230°C/450°F/Gas Mark 8 for twenty minutes. Then cover the pastry to prevent further browning, and continue to bake for a further fifteen minutes. If the fillet is a thick one, this will give you a medium rare middle. If the fillet is from the thin end, give it twenty-five minutes in total. Allow a total of sixty minutes' cooking time for well-done meat.

Fillet steak Carpaccio

This recipe is for lovers of rare or raw beef. Many people who balk at the idea of steak tartare or other raw meat dishes have greatly enjoyed this. Because the beef is cut wafer-thin, 3 or 4 oz (85 or 110 g) of meat for each person is ample. Classically lightly smoked or cured beef is used but we have found ordinary fillet unbeatable.

Fillet steak, cut across the grain into paper-thin slices

For the sauce:
3 tablespoons yogurt
3 tablespoons double
  cream
3 tablespoons
  mayonnaise
1 tablespoon made
  English mustard
Freshly ground black
  pepper, salt
About ½ teaspoon
  creamed horseradish
Squeeze lemon

Put the slices of beef between two pieces of greaseproof paper, and using a mallet or rolling pin beat out the meat until it is as thin as possible. Lay the pieces of steak on the dinner plates as you would smoked salmon, to cover the plate completely but without overlapping.

Mix the first four ingredients for the sauce together, then flavour to taste with the rest of the ingredients. Hand the sauce round separately.

Fillet steak with green peppercorn sauce

In the early seventies in London green peppercorns had a kind of boom in the gastronomic world. But like most passions they did not last long, and are seldom seen today on menus. This is a pity because their flavour is truly delicious – very aromatic and strong, but without the harshness and

The steaks should be at room temperature before frying. Heat a tablespoon of butter in a thick frying pan and when foaming lay the steaks in it. Fry rapidly until very brown on both sides. For rare steaks continue cooking another minute or two on each side, for medium to well-done steaks allow four minutes a side. As soon as the steaks are done to your satisfaction (if you cannot tell by pressing with your thumb – the softer the steak feels the rarer it is – make a small cut in the meat and take a look), pour in the brandy, set it alight and when

scratchiness of dried peppercorns.

4 6-oz (170-g) fillet
  steaks
2 oz (55 g) butter
1 tablespoon brandy
2 tablespoons green
  peppercorns, either
  tinned or frozen
¼ pint (150 ml) double
  cream
Salt, pepper

the flames die down remove the steaks to a warmed serving dish while you make the sauce.

Add the green peppercorns to the pan (if they are frozen they can be added straight from the pack but if they are tinned they should be drained first). Pour in the cream. Boil up the sauce, scraping the bottom of the pan with a wooden spoon. Taste and add salt and pepper if necessary. Pour the sauce over the steaks and serve at once.

Serves 4

Kidney and mushroom vol-au-vent

The cooked kidney mixture will freeze well. Thaw before reheating. For a less strong kidney flavour substitute small chipolata sausages for half the kidneys.

1 family-size vol-au-vent
  (see seafood recipe
  p. 89)
1 lb (450 g) lamb's
  kidneys, skinned,
  halved, and with the
  cores removed
½ lb (225 g) button
  mushrooms, quartered
6 or 8 button onions,
  peeled
About 1½ oz (45 g) butter
2 tablespoons sherry
1 tablespoon tomato
  purée
¾ oz (20 g) flour
12 fluid oz (345 ml) stock
Bouquet garni: bay leaf,
  stick celery, few
  parsley stalks and a
  sprig of thyme, tied
  together with string
Salt, pepper
¼ pint (150 ml) carton sour
  cream
Chopped parsley

Melt half the butter in a shallow saucepan or large sauté pan. Fry a few kidneys, skinned side down, as rapidly as possible. They must brown, not simmer. When brown turn them over, fry the other side, then lift out onto a plate. Repeat, adding more butter, until all the kidneys are done. Fry the onions, then the mushrooms similarly. Put everything back in the pan, but do not add the blood which will have run from the kidneys – it may be bitter.

Pour in the sherry and set it alight. If it won't burn, no matter. When the flames, if any, have died down sprinkle in the flour and add the tomato purée. Mix well, then pour in the stock. Stir until boiling. Add salt and pepper and the bouquet garni. Cover with a lid. Simmer for thirty-five to forty-five minutes or until the onions and kidneys are very tender. If the sauce is on the thin side, strain it into another pan or saucepan, and boil rapidly until it is the consistency of cream. (In any event, remove the bouquet garni.) Taste and add salt and pepper if needed.

Heat the vol-au-vent case and put it on a warm dish. When ready to serve, fill the pastry case with the kidney stew and most of the sauce. Spoon a few generous dollops of sour cream on top, and sprinkle with chopped parsley. Serve at once, handing the extra sauce separately.

Serves 4

Sweetbreads in cream and Calvados

The sweetbread mixture can be made in advance and kept chilled for a day, or frozen if to be kept longer. Thaw completely before reheating. Pastry cases such as vol-au-vents (recipe p. 89) may be used instead of the bread if the party warrants something grander than a toast base.

1 lb (450 g) sweetbreads, preferably calves'
½ chicken stock cube
1½ oz (45 g) butter
1 medium onion, finely chopped
1 dessert apple
½ lb (225 g) white button mushrooms, sliced
3 tablespoons Calvados
1 tablespoon flour
¼ pint (150 ml) dry white wine
Salt, freshly ground white pepper
2 tablespoons double cream
Squeeze lemon juice
4 slices white bread without the crusts
Extra butter for frying the bread

Serves 4

Soak the sweetbreads in successive changes of cold water for two or three hours or until the water is no longer coloured pink. Transfer them to a saucepan and cover with boiling water. Bring to the boil again and simmer for six minutes. Drain them, reserving the liquid. As soon as the sweetbreads are cool enough to handle remove any membrane or sinewy parts. Keep the hot sweetbreads covered so that they cannot dry out. Put the reserved liquid into a saucepan and again bring to the boil. Skim off any scum and add half a chicken stock cube. Boil the stock rapidly until reduced to about 7 fluid oz (200 ml). Set aside.

Melt the butter in a frying pan and gently cook the chopped onion until soft and just beginning to colour. Peel the apple and cut it into small pieces. Fry with the onion until lightly browned and partly softened. With a perforated spoon lift out the apple and onion and put on one side.

Pat the sweetbreads dry, add a little more butter to the pan if necessary and fry the sweetbreads on all sides. They should turn colour slightly but care must be taken not to break them up. After two or three minutes add the sliced mushrooms, with more butter if necessary, and turn the heat up for two minutes or until the mushrooms are cooked. Pour in the Calvados, stand back slightly, and set a match to the pan. When the flames have died down sprinkle in the flour and stir gently until it is evenly distributed.

Pour in the white wine and the reduced sweetbread stock. Stir steadily until simmering point is reached, then add salt (if necessary) and pepper to taste and cover with a lid. Simmer very gently for fifteen minutes. With a perforated spoon lift the solid ingredients out of the pan and allow the liquid to boil rapidly until a thick creamy sauce is achieved. Stir in the double cream, and add a squeeze of lemon juice.

Heat enough butter in a frying pan to fry the four pieces of crustless bread until crisp and golden on both sides. Dish the bread on a heated serving platter and spoon the sweetbreads on top. When ready put the onion and apple into the sauce, simmer for two or three minutes to soften the apple, then spoon the sauce all over the sweetbreads and serve at once.

Braised ox tongue with sour plum sauce

This recipe can be prepared largely in advance – the tongue boiled, and the sauce made – leaving only the slicing and heating of the tongue for the last minute.

1 small salted ox tongue
1 large onion, peeled
4 cloves
Bay leaf, stick of celery, sprig of thyme, few parsley stalks

For the sauce:
1 tablespoon dripping
1 large carrot, finely chopped
1 medium onion, finely chopped
2 teaspoons flour
1 tablespoon tomato purée
1 teaspoon beef extract or Marmite
½ pint (290 ml) beef stock or stock in which the tongue was cooked
½ lb (225 g) stoned red plums stewed in a cupful of water with 3 tablespoons sugar (or 1 small tin plums)
1 tablespoon wine vinegar
1 tablespoon Madeira
Salt, pepper

Serves 6

Ask your butcher if the tongue is very salty. If it is, soak it in a bucket of cold water overnight.

Next day stick the cloves into the peeled onion. Put it with the ox tongue into a saucepan, cover with water and add the herbs and celery stick. Simmer for two or three hours or until tender. Some tongues cook faster than others so check after two hours (a pressure cooker would reduce cooking time to perhaps one hour). Leave the tongue in the hot stock while you make the sauce.

Check the seasoning of the tongue stock. If it is excessively salty it cannot be used, in which case make up some beef stock with a bouillon cube.

Melt the dripping in a heavy saucepan and fry the carrot and onion slowly until they are soft and well browned all over – this may take as much as forty minutes. Stir in the flour, the tomato purée, the beef extract and stock. Bring to the boil, stirring all the time. Simmer until the liquid is reduced to about ½ pint (290 ml) – about forty minutes. Drain into a clean saucepan, add the cooked stoned plums, with not more than a tablespoon of their syrup. Add the wine vinegar, the Madeira, and salt and pepper to taste.

Lift the hot tongue from the stock and carefully skin it. Slice the tongue and arrange it on a heated serving platter. Spoon the sauce and plums over the tongue slices.

Braised oxtail with flageolets

Tinned flageolets are very good. Alternatively small fresh French beans may be used: cook them in boiling salted water until just tender, drain them and add to the stew at the last minute. The oxtail stew itself keeps a week in the refrigerator, and freezes well too, though the meat is inclined to be shreddy on reheating. Do not add the beans until reheating.

Heat the dripping in a heavy large shallow saucepan and fry the oxtail, a few pieces at a time, until well browned all over. Lift onto a plate. Then fry the onions, until evenly browned, lift them out, and fry the carrots. Put everything back and sprinkle in the flour. Mix well and add the tomato purée, the wine, and the stock. Stir until boiling. Sink the bouquet garni in the liquid and season with salt and pepper. Transfer to a cool oven (150°C/300°F/Gas Mark 2) and cook for four hours or until the meat is meltingly tender. Skim any fat from the liquid. Five minutes before serving gently stir in the beans, remove the bouquet garni, check the seasoning, and reheat.

8 good-sized pieces oxtail
½ lb (225 g) carrots, peeled and sliced
½ lb (225 g) onions, sliced
1 or 2 tablespoons beef dripping
1 heaped tablespoon flour
1 tablespoon tomato purée
¼ pint (150 ml) red wine
1 pint (570 ml) beef stock
Bouquet garni: few sprigs parsley, sprig thyme, bay leaf and piece of celery, tied together with string
Salt, pepper
1 small tin flageolet beans, rinsed and drained

Serves 4

Ox tongue with spinach and Madeira wine sauce

Ox tongue is one of the gastronomic joys that has become rarer and rarer in recent years. The old-fashioned way of serving it on a bed of spinach

Ask your butcher if the tongue is very salty. If it is, soak it in a bucket of cold water overnight.

Next day stick the cloves into the peeled onion. Put it with the ox tongue in a saucepan, cover with water and add the herbs and

with a thin Madeira
sauce is still the best.

1 small salted ox tongue
1 lb (450 g) fresh spinach,
  with stalks removed
About 1 oz (30 g) butter
1 large onion, peeled
4 cloves
Bay leaf, stick celery,
  sprig thyme, few
  parsley stalks

For the sauce:
2 oz (55 g) butter
¾ oz (20 g) flour
½ pint (290 ml) beef stock
  or the liquid in which
  the tongue was cooked
3 tablespoons Madeira
Pepper, possibly salt

Serves 6

celery stick. Simmer for two or three hours, or until tender. Some tongues cook faster than others so check after two hours. (A pressure cooker would reduce cooking time to perhaps one hour.) Leave the tongue in the hot stock while you make the sauce.

To make the sauce melt ¾ oz (20 g) of the butter destined for the sauce. Stir in the flour. Cook for half a minute. If the tongue stock is excessively salty it cannot be used and beef stock made with a bouillon cube will have to do instead. Blend in the ½ pint (290 ml) of stock and the Madeira, and stir until boiling. Simmer for ten minutes, and if too thin reduce by rapid boiling. Whisk in the remaining butter bit by bit with the pan held over a moderate heat. Taste, adding pepper if necessary. It is unlikely to need salt.

Cook the spinach in a little boiling salted water until it is reduced in bulk and bright green (about two minutes). Drain it and squeeze out as much water as you can. Spread the spinach on a serving-dish, brush it liberally with butter and season with salt and pepper. Keep warm.

Lift the tongue from the hot stock, skin it and slice it neatly. Lay the slices on top of the spinach, pour over the hot Madeira sauce and serve at once.

Steak with beef marrow and wine sauce

Steaks cannot be kept warm for long without becoming tough and dry, so have the ingredients for the sauce ready before frying the steaks. The actual saucemaking takes only five minutes or so, and if preferred can be made in a second frying pan *while* the steaks are cooking. If this is done make sure the sediment and juices remaining in the steak pan are boiled up (use a little of the wine, or a splash of water) and mixed into the sauce.   PL

4 well-trimmed steaks cut from the rump, sirloin or fillet
2 teaspoons flour
3 oz (85 g) butter
4 shallots, very finely chopped
2 oz (55 g) raw beef marrow, finely sliced
¼ lb (110 g) white button mushrooms
½ pint (290 ml) red wine
Good pinch fresh thyme, or a little dried thyme
Freshly ground black pepper, salt
1 tablespoon chopped parsley

Serves 4

Put the steaks on a board and allow them to come to room temperature. Grind black pepper all over them, pressing it well into the meat so that it sticks. Boil the wine rapidly until reduced by half.

Heat half the butter in a heavy frying pan until foaming and lay the steaks in it. Fry them very fast, browning them on both sides. When they are well browned turn the heat down and continue frying more gently, until the steaks are cooked to your liking. A ½ in (1 cm) thick steak will take about four minutes per side for a medium, pinkish, steak; a rare one will obviously take less and a well-done one a total of about twelve minutes.

Add the rest of the butter to the pan, add the shallots and beef marrow, and fry for one minute. Add the mushrooms. Cook one more minute. Stir in the flour, then the wine, thyme, pepper and parsley, and boil up well. Add salt to taste and tip over the steaks.

Ices,
Puddings
&
Desserts

Ices and Desserts

Very rich vanilla ice-cream

This is the richest of true ice-creams. Not for the calorie-conscious or the cholesterol-conscious, it contains real cream, real eggs and plenty of sugar. However, it tastes like ice-cream used to taste once upon a time.

1 pint (570 ml) milk
½ pint (290 ml) single cream
½ lb (225 g) castor sugar
8 egg yolks
Few drops vanilla essence

Serves 5–6

Set the freezer or ice compartment to coldest. Put the milk, cream and sugar into a heavy saucepan and bring slowly to the boil. Beat the yolks with the vanilla essence in a large bowl. Pour the boiling milky mixture from a height onto the yolks, whisking as you do so. Strain into a roasting pan or into two ice-trays. Cool. Freeze until solid but still soft enough to give when pressed with a finger. Tip the ice-cream into a cold bowl, break it up, then whisk with a rotary beater until smooth, pale and creamy. If you have a food processor like a Magimix, all the better. Refreeze.

If the ice-cream is made more than six hours in advance it will be hard to scoop. Put it in the refrigerator for one hour before serving to allow it to soften.

Pistachio ice-cream

Make the very rich vanilla ice-cream (recipe above), adding ¼ lb (110 g) finely chopped or ground pistachio nuts before the final whisking.

Serves 5–6

Coffee ice-cream

Make the very rich vanilla ice-cream (recipe above), adding coffee essence (about two tablespoons Camp or 1 tablespoon instant coffee mixed with one tablespoon boiling water) during the final whisking. A marvellous grainy texture and pure coffee flavour are given by the addition of a tablespoon of pure finely ground coffee, added dry, as well as the liquid coffee essence.

Serves 5–6

Mint ice-cream

Make the very rich vanilla ice-cream (recipe p. 143), adding a few sprigs of mint to flavour the heating cream and milk, and a few drops of mint or peppermint essence and a drop of green colouring to the final custard.

Serves 5–6

Mincemeat ice-cream

Follow the very rich vanilla ice-cream (recipe p. 143) adding a jar of mincemeat (the Christmas mince-pie kind) and a dash of brandy or rum before freezing the first time.

Serves 5–6

Vanilla and chestnut ice-cream with apricot and rum sauce

Follow the very rich vanilla ice-cream (recipe p. 143). During the final whisking beat in $\frac{1}{4}$ lb (110 g) finely chopped candied chestnuts.

To make the sauce heat together $\frac{1}{2}$ lb (225 g) sieved apricot jam, $\frac{1}{4}$ pint (150 ml) water, and a squeeze of lemon. Stir until smooth. Boil until syrupy, then add a tablespoon of rum.

Serves 5–6

Vanilla ice-cream with passionfruit

The sweet but tart flavour of granadillas is wonderful with rich sweet vanilla ice-cream. Everything can be made in advance. Remember to remove the ice-cream from freezer to refrigerator just before dinner to give it time to soften slightly.

$\frac{1}{2}$ pint (290 ml) passion-fruit pulp (tinned is fine)
2 tablespoons sherry
Castor sugar to taste
Vanilla ice-cream
  (recipe p. 143)

Mix together the passionfruit, sherry and enough castor sugar to sweeten. Put this mixture into a jug and hand round with the ice-cream.

Serves 5–6

Strawberry ice-cream

The greatest bore about ice-cream making, if you do not have an ice-cream machine, is the half-time rewhisking usually necessary to get a creamy smooth result. This ice-cream, happily, doesn't need it, but without a mixing machine that will whip egg whites it is hard work on the beating arm.

¼ pint (150 ml) water
½ lb (225 g) castor sugar
2 large egg whites
Juice and finely grated rind of 1 small orange
1 lb (450 g) strawberries, pushed through a sieve
½ pint (290 ml) double cream

Dissolve the sugar in the water and bring to the boil. When clear boil steadily for five minutes. While the syrup is bubbling beat the whites to a stiff snow. When the syrup boiling time is up pour it onto the whites, whisking as you do so. Keep whisking until you have a thick meringue. Stir in the rind, orange juice and strawberry purée. Whip the cream until thick but not quite solid. Fold it in and freeze.

Serves 6–8

Raspberry ice-cream

Follow the strawberry ice-cream recipe (above), substituting raspberries for strawberries.

Serves 6–8

Rhubarb ice-cream

Follow the strawberry ice-cream recipe (above), substituting cooked, sweetened and puréed rhubarb for the strawberries.

Serves 6–8

Greengage ice-cream

Follow the strawberry ice-cream recipe (above), substituting cooked, slightly sweetened and puréed greengages for the strawberries, and omitting the orange rind and juice. Add a few drops green colouring.

Serves 6–8

Damson ice-cream

Follow the strawberry ice-cream recipe (p. 145), substituting cooked, slightly sweetened and puréed damsons for the strawberries, and omitting the orange rind and juice.

Serves 6–8

Pear creams

These little pots of creamy pear mousse owe their beautiful flavour to the fact that the pears are raw. They have a really fresh taste which puts them above the average cold mousse.

4 egg yolks
1 large or 2 small ripe pears
2 oz (55 g) castor sugar
4 fluid oz (110 ml) double cream
1 tablespoon apricot jam
$\frac{1}{3}$ oz (10 g) powdered gelatine, soaked in 3 tablespoons water

Serves 4

Peel, core and liquidize (or sieve) the pears with half the sugar. Half-whip the cream. Put the yolks, the rest of the sugar, and two tablespoons of water into the top of a double boiler or into a bowl fixed over a pan of simmering water. Whisk over gentle heat until thick, light and pale. Remove from the heat and keep whisking while gently heating the gelatine in a small pan. When the gelatine is runny and clear stir it into the egg mixture, then stir in the puréed pears, and finally the cream. Pour into four ramekin dishes. Allow to set in the fridge.

When the mousse is set melt the jam with the water and sieve it. Use it to coat the top of each mousse.

Passionfruit syllabub

This isn't a real syllabub but we don't know what to call it. Incidentally, it makes a wonderful sauce for left-over Christmas pudding.

$\frac{1}{2}$ pint (290 ml) double cream, softly whipped
2 tablespoons sweet sherry
$\frac{1}{3}$ pint (190 ml) sweetened passionfruit pulp (fresh is best but tinned will do)

Flavour the cream with the sherry. Put a spoonful into each of four tall glasses. Add a spoonful of passionfruit, then one of cream and so on until the mixture is finished. Chill well.

Serves 4

Ginger cream

The recipe for this syllabub-like cream is often requested by customers at Leith's. I'm always faintly ashamed to produce such childishly simple instructions, when the diner obviously thinks there is some magical method or mysterious ingredient to it.

½ pint (290 ml) whipped cream
¼ pint (150 ml) ginger marmalade
¼ pint (150 ml) Advokaat

Mix together the whipped cream, ginger marmalade (sieved if you want a smooth cream) and the Advokaat. Chill well and serve in small individual pots or as a sauce for a melony fruit salad.

Serves 4

Greek fruit salad with ice

This is so fresh and simple it should be served all summer long. You need to provide each guest with a finger-bowl and big napkin, preferably a cloth one.

Wipe or wash fruit as you would for fruit salad, but leave the pieces large enough to pick up in the fingers comfortably – bananas in quarters, for example; pineapple in long fingers; two or three grapes in a tiny bunch; cherries with their stalks intact; strawberries unhulled; apples cut into eighths, etc.

Arrange the fruit on a large deep platter, cover with plastic wrap and chill well. (If the fruit is likely to discolour, chill it whole and peel and cut before serving.)

Tip a bowlful of crushed ice or small ice cubes all over the fruit just before taking it to the table.

Mangoes in orange juice

Peel ripe small mangoes. Slice them in thickish large slices, not small segments (they look like tinned peaches if you do that). Sprinkle them liberally with orange juice and sparingly with castor sugar and chill for an hour or so before serving.

Figs and pears in orange juice

This is a glorified fruit salad, but when pears are in season it is one of the nicest ways of serving them.

Ripe figs, preferably the
　　greeny-yellow kind
Ripe pears, preferably
　　the juicy Bartlett kind
Orange juice
Castor sugar

Peel the figs and cut them into quarters, laying them in a glass dish. Peel the pears and add them to the figs, arranging them attractively. Sprinkle liberally with castor sugar and with the orange juice. Chill well.

Pears in burgundy

Many cooks prefer to cook the pears whole for this recipe, leaving on the stalks. It is true that this looks pretty but it requires double the amount of wine and syrup in order to keep the pears well covered during cooking. However, the syrup may be used again and again, keeping for weeks in the refrigerator. The pears should be poached on the day of serving; they become dull-coloured if kept overnight, though they still taste very good.

4 large ripe Bartlett pears
½ pint (290 ml) burgundy
　　or similar red wine
¼ lb (110 g) castor sugar
1 cinnamon stick
Rind of 1 lemon

Serves 4

Put the wine, sugar, cinnamon and lemon rind together in a wide shallow saucepan and bring slowly to the boil, stirring occasionally. Peel the pears, cut them in half, and with a teaspoon scoop out the core. As soon as the pears are peeled and halved, drop them into the hot syrup. Bring rapidly to the boil and allow to boil fairly fast so that the bubbles cover the pears. After four or five minutes turn the heat down and simmer gently until the pears are slightly glassy looking and very well cooked. If the syrup is thin remove the pears and boil the liquid fast until the required consistency is reached. Allow them to cool in their syrup, then tip into a glass dish.

Peppermint pears

These pears may be prepared two or three days in advance and kept refrigerated. Do not freeze.

4 large ripe perfect pears
½ pint (290 ml) water
5 oz (140 g) sugar
Finely pared rind 1 lemon
2 or 3 drops green colouring
Peppermint essence
2 or 3 sprigs mint

Serves 4

Put the sugar, water, lemon rind and mint leaves in a saucepan and bring slowly to the boil, stirring occasionally. Once the syrup is clear and boiling peel the pears, cut them in half and using a teaspoon remove the cores. Drop them, as soon as they are peeled, into the boiling syrup. Boil rapidly for three or four minutes so that the bubbles completely cover the pears: this will prevent discolouring. Simmer the pears until well cooked and almost transparent – about forty minutes. Colour the syrup delicately with a little green colouring and flavour to taste with a few drops peppermint essence. Tip into a glass bowl and chill well before serving.

Lemon mousse

This classic mousse freezes to perfection. Allow to thaw overnight in the refrigerator or larder, then decorate with the cream and nuts.

3 eggs, separated
5 oz (140 g) castor sugar
¼ oz (8 g) powdered gelatine
3 tablespoons water
Juice and very finely grated rind 2 medium-sized lemons
Slightly less than ½ pint (290 ml) double cream, lightly whipped
2-3 tablespoons browned chopped almonds, or chopped walnuts

Serves 4

Put the gelatine and the water into a small saucepan and leave to soak for ten minutes or so. Put the yolks and sugar in a mixing bowl and whisk with an electric machine until stiff, gradually adding the lemon juice and rind as you go. (Failing a machine set the bowl over a saucepan of simmering water and whisk with a hand wire whisk or a rotary beater. Once thick and mousse-like remove the bowl from the heat, stand it in cold water and continue to whisk until the mixture has cooled.)

Set the soaked gelatine over gentle heat until it is runny and clear. Stir briskly into the egg and lemon mixture, until the mixture begins to thicken and set. Now stir in half the double cream. Quickly whisk the three egg whites until snowy and stiff but not dry looking. Fold them into the mixture and tip it into a serving dish. Resist the temptation to over-stir: a few pockets of air are preferable to a mousse which has been over-mixed and lost most of its fluffiness. Allow to set in the refrigerator. Use the rest of the whipped cream and the nuts for decoration.

Peaches in brandy

If the peaches are large and perfect in shape, as well as absolutely ripe, they should be treated as below. If, however, they are on the hard side, or are at all damaged, they should be peeled and gently poached in the syrup until cooked through. If they are to be served raw, as below, they should not be prepared more than three hours before serving.

4 perfect ripe peaches
5 oz (140 g) sugar
½ pint (290 ml) water
2 tablespoons brandy
Juice of ½ lemon

Serves 4

Dip the peaches into boiling water for ten seconds and remove the skins. Place the peeled peaches in a glass serving-dish and chill well. Boil the sugar and water together to form a tacky syrup. Add the juice of half a lemon and the brandy. Pour over the peaches and chill well.

Pears in crème de menthe

This fresh and minty compôte is very pretty, and is simple to do. Can be made the day before.

4 ripe perfect pears
6 oz (170 g) sugar
½ pint (290 ml) water
3 tablespoons crème de menthe
Juice and rind 1 lemon
A little green colouring

Serves 4

Put the finely pared lemon rind, the sugar and the water together in a saucepan of the size to take neatly the four whole pears. Heat the sugar and water gently until dissolved, then boil rapidly for a minute or two. Peel the pears, leaving them whole, with the stalks intact. Use a teaspoon to scoop out the flower end of the stalk. Put the pears into the boiling syrup and cover with a lid and boil up rapidly so that the bubbles cover the fruit: this will prevent discolouring. Cook the pears until they are almost glassy in appearance and cooked right through – about forty minutes. Lift them out and put them in a glass serving bowl, standing on their fat ends. Add the lemon juice to the syrup with the crème de menthe, and enough green colouring to tint the syrup delicately. Strain the syrup over the pears and chill well before serving.

Pineapple rice condé

This is a delicious and luxurious edition of rice pudding. It sounds fiddly to do but is in fact fairly quick and very easy. It cannot be frozen.

For the rice pudding:
2 oz (55 g) pudding rice
1 pint (570 ml) milk
½ oz (15 g) butter
1½ oz (45 g) castor sugar
2 drops vanilla essence

¼ pint (150 ml) double
   cream, whipped
1 medium-sized pineapple
2 oz (55 g) castor sugar
2 tablespoons Kirsch
2 tablespoons apricot jam

Serves 4–5

Put all the ingredients for the rice pudding into a pie-dish and cook them in a low oven (about 150°C; 300°F; gas mark 2) until the pudding is almost set. This might take as much as three hours, and it is a good idea to stir the pudding once in a while, partly to break up the skin and partly to encourage even cooking. Once the pudding is made take it out of the oven and allow it to cool completely.

Meanwhile cut the top off the pineapple and keep it for decoration. Remove its skin and cut the flesh into very thin, even slices. Put these in a bowl with the castor sugar and Kirsch. Leave to macerate in the fridge for about six hours.

When the pudding is cold and the pineapple slices macerated lift the slices out of their juice and put the juice in a saucepan with the apricot jam. Stir over gentle heat until melted and smooth, then push through a sieve. Allow to cool to tepid.

Tip the rice pudding into a large bowl and beat well with a fork or whisk. Whip the cream until stiff but not quite solid and fold into the rice. You should now have a soft, creamy but just solid mixture. Choose a large, flat, oval dish and put the rice on it. Shape it into a shallow oval. Flatten the top as best you can. With the handle of a teaspoon mark fairly deep grooves in the rice pudding in a diagonal lattice pattern to resemble the skin of a pineapple. Put the rice pudding in the freezer to chill for ten or fifteen minutes.

Take the pineapple top and cut it in half. Wash one half. Once the rice pudding is chilled, and the apricot glaze is almost cold, set the pineapple top at the end of the pudding to form the leafy end of the rice 'pineapple'. Carefully spoon the just-liquid apricot glaze all over the pudding. It should run into the grooves made with the teaspoon, so accentuating the 'pineapple look' of the dish. Serve the slices of pineapple in a separate bowl, to be eaten with the pudding.

Vacherin with grapes and chestnuts

The meringue base can be made weeks in advance, and kept in an airtight plastic bag until needed. Do not assemble the cake more than four hours in advance or the meringue may become too soft. Alternative fillings such as whipped cream and raspberries, or pineapple, walnuts and whipped cream, or lemon curd and whipped cream, etc., may be substituted for the grapes and chestnuts.

3 egg whites
6 oz (170 g) castor sugar
1 teaspoon vinegar
½ lb (225 g) green grapes
1 small tin candied
  chestnuts
¼ pint (150 ml) double
  cream

Serves 6–8

First make the meringue. Whisk the egg whites until stiff and dry looking. Add half the sugar and the vinegar and keep whisking until once again you have a stiff, almost solid, mixture. Fold in the rest of the sugar. Lightly brush a large piece of foil with oil. Sprinkle lightly with castor sugar. Using a piping bag or large spoon spread the meringue mixture evenly on the foil so that you have a round disc about the size of a dessert plate and 1 in or ¾ in (2½ cm or 2 cm) thick.

Set the oven at 100°C/200°F/Gas Mark ½, and put the meringue into it to dry out completely. This should take about two hours, by which time it should be easy to peel the foil off the back of the meringue disc without breaking it. If the foil sticks the meringue is not yet ready and needs further baking. Once the meringue is cool put it on a serving-dish. Whip the double cream until stiff and spread all over the meringue.

Split the grapes in half and remove the seeds. Cut the chestnuts into halves or quarters and arrange grapes and chestnuts all over the cream. Sprinkle the vacherin with a little of the syrup from the tin of chestnuts.

Milles feuilles

This is one of those cakes that is seldom attempted at home although it is very easy to make, especially if you use bought puff pastry, which works perfectly well. The trick is to bake the puff pastry until really crisp and cooked right through. The pastry may be baked in advance and stored overnight in an airtight bag. But the cake should not be assembled more than four hours before eating.

Roll the puff pastry out very thinly and cut it into four even-sized strips measuring roughly 10 by 4 in (25 by 10 cm) each. Prick the pieces all over and put on baking sheets. Heat the oven to 230°C/450°F/Gas Mark 8. Bake the pastry until very crisp and brown – about twenty minutes. Turn the pieces of pastry over and put back in the oven to ensure brownness and crispness. Allow to cool while you whip the double cream until stiff.

Take the best piece of puff pastry and set aside. Put one of the other pieces on a board and spread it all over with jam. Then spread with a third of the double cream. Put another piece of pastry on the top and again spread it with jam and then cream. Repeat with the third piece and then put the reserve piece on top.

1 lb (450 g) puff pastry
½ pint (290 ml) double
  cream
4 tablespoons strawberry
  or raspberry jam
¼ lb (110 g) icing sugar
A little boiling water
3 oz (85 g) chopped
  almonds, browned
  under the grill

Serves 6

With your hands press the pile of pastry and filling down firmly. This is important or the whole thing will fall to bits when it is cut. Using a bread knife trim the edges of the pastry evenly to neaten up the cake. Sift the icing sugar into a bowl and beat in enough boiling water to get a smooth, just runny, icing. Spoon this all over the top sheet of pastry. Sprinkle the nuts carefully down the long edges of the cake while the icing is still wet.

When serving cut the mille feuilles across in 1 in (2½ cm) slices.

Classic chocolate mousse

This recipe relies on the large quantity of chocolate to set the mousse to a soft but not solid consistency. It is very rich, but contains no sugar. Set it in small individual ramekins or coffee cups rather than in a large dish. It is best made the day before eating but can be made three days in advance. The mousse can be flavoured with brandy, strong coffee essence or grated orange rind. It may also be served with whipped cream heavily flavoured with ginger syrup from a preserved ginger jar.

¼ lb (110 g) plain good
   quality chocolate
½ oz (15 g) butter
4 medium-sized eggs

Chop up the chocolate on a board and put it in the top of a double saucepan or on a bowl set over a saucepan of simmering water. Simmer the water slowly until the chocolate has melted, giving it an occasional stir. Take the chocolate off the heat, stir in the butter and, provided the chocolate is not too hot (which it should not be), beat in the egg yolks only. Whisk the egg whites until stiff, then fold them into the melted chocolate and yolk mixture. Pour the mousse immediately into individual dishes and refrigerate until set, preferably overnight.

Serves 4

Italian meringue pie

A lovely looking cake – like a Queen Mum hat. The outside is soft meringue with a good boozy middle. Keeps a day or two and freezes well.

1 large all-in-one cake (recipe below) or plain bought sponge
1 small tin black cherries, with stones removed
¼ pint (150 ml) double cream, stiffly whipped
1 tablespoon rum
2 egg whites
4½ oz (125 g) icing sugar
2 drops vanilla essence

Serves 6

With a sharp skewer make holes in the sponge cake so that when you pour the syrup onto it later it will penetrate easily. Split the cake in half, using a bread knife. Mix the whipped cream with the drained cherries (keep the juice from the cherry can). Put the bottom layer of the cake on a heatproof serving-dish and sprinkle it evenly with the rum. Then sprinkle enough of the black cherry juice over it to dampen it well without soaking it completely – it should be patchy. Spread the cream and cherries on this and cover the pudding with the top layer of cake. Set the oven to 200°C/400°F/Gas Mark 6.

If you have a robust mixing machine use it to beat the egg whites until stiff, then add the sugar and vanilla and whisk to a very solid meringue. Failing a machine put the whites, sugar and vanilla into a large bowl and set it over a saucepan of simmering water, making sure that the bottom of the mixing bowl does not touch the surface of the water. Using a rotary beater or a hand whisk beat the meringue until stiff. Use a palette knife to spread this meringue all over the cake. Bake in the oven for ten minutes or until the meringue is lightly coloured. Allow to cool before serving.

All-in-one cake

¼ lb (110 g) self-raising flour
1 level teaspoon baking powder
¼ lb (110 g) soft margarine (the kind bought in tubs)
¼ lb (110 g) castor sugar
2 eggs
Grated rind ½ lemon
2 drops vanilla essence
Melted butter for greasing cake tin

While the oven is heating to 170°C/325°F/Gas Mark 3, get the cake tin ready. It should be 8 in (20 cm) in diameter and about 1¾ in (4½ cm) deep. Cut paper to fit the bottom of the tin and brush the sides and the paper with melted butter. Put all the ingredients together in a mixing bowl and whisk for a minute if you have an electric whisk, or until everything is well mixed and smooth. Spoon into the cake tin and level off the top. Bake in the middle of the oven for half an hour. When the cake feels firm to the touch and looks very slightly shrunken round the edge it is done. Remove and allow to cool for twenty minutes or so in the tin. Tip out upside-down on a wire cooling rack to finish cooling.

Once cold split the cake horizontally with a bread knife and fill with jam or whipped cream for tea, or use for puddings such as the Italian meringue pie (recipe p. 154).

Profiteroles with cream and apricot sauce

Profiteroles are surprisingly easy to make provided the quantities in the recipe are accurately measured, and the instructions followed slavishly. They freeze beautifully filled or unfilled. If they are to be frozen when filled it is best to freeze the empty profiteroles first and fill them while they are in a hard and frozen state. This means that when they thaw they will be crisper than if filled while the pastry is not rigid.

For the choux paste:
3¾ oz (105 g) plain flour
7½ fluid oz (220 ml) water
¼ lb (110 g) butter
3 medium sized eggs
Good pinch salt

For the filling:
Double cream
Castor sugar (optional)
Rum (optional)

Sifted icing sugar
Apricot sauce (recipe
  p. 157)

Serves 6

Put the water and the butter in a wide heavy saucepan and set over gentle heat. Once the butter has melted completely, bring rapidly to the boil. As soon as you have a rolling boil tip in all the flour and stir briskly with a wooden spoon. When the mixture is lump-free and curls away from the side of the saucepan tip it into a large cold bowl, and with a wooden spoon spread it around the sides of the bowl to encourage it to cool.

When the mixture is cold enough to touch with your hand beat in the eggs, one by one. You should end up with a soft mixture of dropping consistency. This means that it will fall off the spoon if given a slight jerk, neither running off too easily nor adhering obstinately to it. It should be smooth and slightly shiny. Beat in the salt.

Put the mixture in small rounded spoonfuls on a baking sheet, making sure the blobs are fairly well apart.

Set the oven to 200°C/400°F/Gas Mark 6, and when it is hot bake the profiteroles for about twenty-five minutes or until firm to the touch and browned. Take them from the oven and immediately split them in half, opening them up to allow the steam to escape, and the insides to dry out.

Whip the cream until thick, and flavour it, if liked, with a little rum and sugar. Fill the profiteroles with this, put back the lids, and arrange them on a serving-dish. Dredge them lightly with icing sugar and serve with a thin apricot sauce, either hot or cold.

Strawberry ring

This is one of the easiest of glamorous puddings. The choux pastry ring can be made well in advance and kept frozen. It may be filled and iced four or five hours before dinner.

The ingredients for choux pastry (see profiteroles recipe p. 155)
½ pint (290 ml) double cream
½ lb (225 g) fresh strawberries
1 tablespoon strawberry jam

For the icing:
¼ lb (110 g) icing sugar
Boiling water

Serves 6

Make up the choux mixture as instructed on p. 155, but instead of piping or spooning it into small balls use a large-nozzled piping bag and pipe a hollow ring about the size of a dessert plate. The sides of the mixture should be about 1 in (2½ cm) high. If using a spoon, spoon the blobs of mixture close together in a circle – don't worry about smoothing the top. It looks good if rather uneven.

Bake at 220°C/425°F/Gas Mark 7, for twenty-five to thirty-five minutes or until well risen and brown, and firm to the touch. As soon as the ring emerges from the oven split it in half horizontally to give a base and a lid of roughly equal size. Scoop out any uncooked paste from the middle, and return the two halves to the oven, inside up, to dry out for five minutes. Cool.

Whip the cream. Cut the strawberries in halves or quarters and mix gently with the cream. Spread the jam in the bottom of the choux pastry base. Fill with the strawberry cream. Put on the lid. Mix the icing sugar with enough boiling water to give a just runny mixture. Spoon over the top of the ring, allowing the icing to trickle down the sides.

Beignet with apricot sauce

A deep-fried version of the profiteroles, really a fritter, particularly good if served with cold apricot sauce, the contrast of hot and cold being very pleasant. The apricot sauce can be ·made in advance and so can the choux paste mixture. This leaves only the last-minute frying to be done.   PL

Choux paste (recipe p. 155)
Apricot sauce
Castor sugar
Oil for deep frying

Follow the profiteroles recipe above exactly, but do not bake the mixture. Instead, heat some very clean fat or oil of a good depth until it will sizzle vigorously when a crumb is dropped into it. Spoon small blobs of the choux paste mixture into the hot oil and fry them fairly fast until risen, puffed up and nicely browned. Lift them out and drain immediately on crumpled kitchen paper. Roll them in castor sugar and serve at once with a cold apricot sauce (recipe p. 157).

Serves 5–6

Apricot sauce

This sauce is really an old English jam sauce. It is wonderfully useful for bland puddings or pastries which need something strong-tasting and sweet to liven them up. It is equally good for rich and sweet desserts like ice-cream which need something slightly tart to go with them.

For hot sauce:
Put four tablespoons of thick apricot jam into a heavy-bottomed saucepan with about ¼ pint (150 ml) of water. Stir slowly until the jam has melted, and boil the sauce to a syrupy consistency. For a smooth texture push through a fine sieve.

For cold sauce:
Proceed as above but use three tablespoons of jam, ⅓ pint (190 ml) of water and a tablespoon of sugar.

If the apricot sauce, on cooling, has become very solid or thick it should be liquidized or blended with a little water or sugar syrup.

Rum and coffee cake

This is ridiculously simple, but very rich.

2 large plain sponge cakes or 2 boxes 'trifle' sponges*
3 heaped tablespoons instant coffee
4 tablespoons castor sugar
7 fluid oz (200 ml) water
1 tablespoon rum

For the icing:
3 oz (85 g) unsalted butter
6 oz (170 g) icing sugar
⅓ pint (190 ml) double cream
2 oz (55 g) whole toasted almonds

Serves 6

Boil the water. Add the sugar and stir until dissolved. Add the rum and the coffee. Break up the cakes roughly. Pour over the coffee mixture. Stir, without mixing at all thoroughly – the cake should be half plain and half coffee-soaked. Tip into a pudding basin, press down well, then turn out onto a plate. (If the cake can be left overnight in the basin with a saucer and a weight compressing it, so much the better.) Beat the butter and icing sugar together until soft, pale and fluffy. Using a knife dipped in hot water spread the icing all over the cake. Whip the cream and completely mask the icing with it. Stick the almonds into the cream like the spines of a hedgehog.

*The All-in-one Cake (recipe p. 154) is a good plain cake. Omit the lemon and add two drops vanilla essence.

Almond pastry fruit flan

This pastry can be made in a flash with one of the new Magimix food processors, but is slightly messy to make by hand. The very short rich crumbly pastry justifies the effort, however. Any fresh fruit may be used for the topping, but it should be chosen with an eye to colour as much as to flavour. The pastry may be cooked in advance and kept in a biscuit tin, but the flan should not be assembled more than three hours before eating, for the pastry is liable to become soggy on standing too long.

For the pastry:
¼ lb (110 g) plain flour
3 oz (85 g) softened butter
Large pinch salt
1½ oz (45 g) castor sugar
Yolk 1 large egg
1½ oz (45 g) ground
 almonds
1 drop almond essence

About 2½ lb (1.15 kg)
 fruit of your choice
 (e.g. 1 large banana,
 ¼ lb (110 g) grapes,
 2 oranges, 1 small tin
 mandarins, 1 large
 pear, 1 small punnet
 strawberries)
3-4 tablespoons apricot
 jam
Juice of ½ lemon

Serves 6

If making the pastry with a machine simply put all the ingredients together and mix until a soft paste is formed. Take care not to over-mix. With floured hands lift out the ball of dough and chill it well before handling further.

If making the pastry by hand proceed as follows. Sift the flour into a large bowl. Make a well in the middle and put the softened butter, pinch of salt, the castor sugar, yolk of egg and drop of almond essence into the middle. With the fingers of one hand mix the central ingredients to a paste and then gradually incorporate the surrounding flour. When everything is almost mixed together add the ground almonds and knead briefly to a smooth ball. Chill well before proceeding.

Set the oven to 200°C/400°F/Gas Mark 6. With your hands press the pastry into a round or oval flat shape not more than ½ in (1 cm) thick. With a fork or your fingers mark the edge in a neat pattern. Bake the pastry until biscuit-coloured in the middle and slightly browner at the edges. Remove from the oven and allow to get almost cold before attempting to remove from the baking sheet. Place the cooled pastry on a serving-dish.

Melt the apricot jam with the juice of the lemon and push it through a sieve. Use this to lightly brush the almond pastry top. Cut the fruit up as you might for fruit salad (e.g. halve the grapes and take the pips out, peel and cut the pear into neat segments, peel the orange as if it was an apple, removing skin and pith at the same time, and separate the segments). Arrange the fruit in neat rows on the pastry, making sure that you do not have two white fruits together or two red fruits together – the colours should be contrasting. Use the rest of the apricot glaze to brush a thin coating all over the fruit. Chill before serving.

Bourdaloue tart with apricots

This classic **French** flan can be varied **endlessly**. Substitute any cooked or fresh fruit for the apricots, using redcurrant jelly for the glaze if the fruit is red. Make on the day of serving. The pastry goes soggy if kept filled for too long, but flan case, custard and glaze can all be prepared the day before, leaving only the assembly for the day of serving. Will not freeze well.

For the pastry:
¼ lb (110 g) flour
A good pinch salt
2 egg yolks
2 oz (55 g) soft butter
2 oz (55 g) sugar
2 drops vanilla essence

For the custard cream:
½ pint (290 ml) milk
2 egg yolks
2 oz (55 g) sugar
½ oz (15 g) flour
1 oz (30 g) cornflour
2 tablespoons ground
  almonds
2 tablespoons double
  cream
2 drops almond essence

For the top:
1 lb (450 g) apricots
  (or tinned ones)
1 tablespoon apricot jam
A little of the syrup from
  cooking the apricots (or
  from the tin if using
  tinned apricots)

Serves 6

Make the pastry first. If using a machine put all the pastry ingredients in together and mix to a soft dough. Take care not to over-mix, and chill well before handling further. If making the pastry by hand sift the flour into a large bowl, make a hole in the centre and drop in the salt, egg yolks, soft butter and vanilla essence. With the fingertips of one hand mix the central ingredients to a smooth paste, then gradually draw in the surrounding flour. When about half the flour is incorporated add the sugar and continue mixing with your hand until you have a smooth paste. Chill before proceeding.

Meanwhile make the custard cream. Put the flour, cornflour and sugar into a medium-sized saucepan and mix in the two egg yolks. Once this is smooth add the ½ pint (290 ml) of milk and bring, stirring, to the boil. Don't worry about the lumps – they will certainly form, but will disappear once the custard is boiling and well stirred. Add the almond essence and the cream and allow to cool. Once cool stir in the ground almonds. Heat the oven to 190°C/ 375°F/Gas Mark 5.

Use the pastry to line a 7 in (18 cm) flan ring or flan dish. Put a piece of tin foil into the flan dish and fill it with rice, dried beans, pebbles or pennies – anything to hold the pastry down while it bakes. Bake for fifteen minutes. Lift out the foil and the weights and return the flan ring to the oven for a further five or ten minutes until the sides are evenly browned and the pastry on the bottom cooked. Allow to cool.

Fill the cold flan case with the cold creamy custard and arrange the drained apricots all over the top. Put the apricot jam and sugar syrup (two to three tablespoons) in a saucepan and heat slowly until the jam is melted. Boil rapidly until you have a thick syrup. Allow to cool until thick but not set. Use this to cover the apricots in a thin glaze.

Almond pastry cases filled with vanilla ice-cream

This recipe sounds more complicated than it is, and *always* causes gasps of admiration. The biscuit cups can be made in advance and stored in an airtight bin. If and when you open the biscuit tin the cups are no longer crisp return them to the oven (again on their inverted teacups, see below) for four or five minutes, then allow to cool again.

Vanilla ice-cream
 (recipe p. 143)

For the pastry cases:
3 oz (85 g) castor sugar
3 oz (85 g) butter
3 eggs
1½ oz (45 g) ground
 almonds
1½ oz (45 g) flour
3 drops almond essence

To serve:
Hot apricot sauce
 (recipe p. 157)

Serves 6

First make the pastry cases. Melt the butter and the sugar together in a medium-sized sauce-pan. Add the almond essence and, once the mixture is not more than tepid, beat in the eggs. Finally mix in the sifted flour and the almonds. Set the oven at 190°C/375°F/Gas Mark 5.

Grease two or three baking sheets and put the pastry mixture in tablespoons on the baking sheets, well apart. With the back of the spoon spread them thinly and evenly into saucer-sized discs. Bake for five minutes or until it is possible to lift the biscuits from the baking sheet with a fish slice. They should be very pliable at this stage but by no means cooked. Put some teacups or oven-proof tumblers upside down on the baking sheet and lay the bendable biscuits over the top of the teacups, moulding them so as to shape them roughly. Return the whole thing, cups and all, to the oven and continue to bake until the biscuits are evenly browned. Allow to cool before removing them from the upside-down teacups. Once cold, store them in an airtight container.

Not more than half an hour before serving put the biscuits onto the serving dish and fill with balls of vanilla ice-cream. Serve with the hot apricot sauce.

Brandy snaps filled with orange cream

Brandy snaps seldom contain brandy, but the sweetened cream filling may be flavoured with brandy, sherry, whisky, or chocolate instead of orange.

Melt the sugar, butter and syrup together in a heavy-bottomed saucepan. Add the flour, ground ginger and lemon juice. Remove from the heat and stir well until smooth. Grease two or three baking sheets lightly with oil and put the mixture on them in teaspoonfuls, well apart. Set the oven to 190°C/375°F/Gas

¼ lb (110 g) butter
¼ lb (110 g) castor sugar
¼ lb (110 g) (or 4 table-
    spoons) golden syrup
¼ lb (110 g) plain flour
½ teaspoon ground ginger
Juice of ½ lemon
Oil for greasing baking
    sheets

For the filling:
Whipped cream
    sweetened with castor
    sugar and flavoured
    with grated orange
    rind

Serves 4

Mark 5, and when hot bake the biscuits for eight or ten minutes or until browned and hard at the edges. Remove from the oven, allow to cool for a minute or so, then lift off with a fish slice or spatula. Shape the brandy snaps round the handle of a large wooden spoon so that they are rolled up and hollow in the middle. Allow to cool completely.

Use a forcing bag and fluted nozzle to fill the brandy snaps with the flavoured cream.

Almond cake

The best of cakes. Rich enough for after dinner and perfection for tea.

2 oz (55 g) potato starch
    or plain flour
½ teaspoon baking
    powder
Good pinch salt
3 oz (85 g) butter
¼ lb (110 g) blanched
    almonds
5 oz (140 g) castor sugar
3 eggs
1 tablespoon Amaretto
    liqueur or Kirsch
Icing sugar

Serves 4–6

Set the oven at 180°C/350°F/Gas Mark 4. Brush an 8 in (20 cm) cake tin lightly with butter, line the bottom with a circle of grease-proof paper and brush the paper too.

In a coffee mill, liquidizer or mortar, grind the almonds finely. Put them into a bowl, and add the eggs one at a time, beating thoroughly until the mixture is pale and thick. Sift the potato starch or flour with the baking powder and salt. Fold it into the mixture, as lightly as possible, with a large metal spoon. Melt the butter, add the liqueur to it and fold it into the cake mixture with the minimum of stirring. Pour the mixture into the cake tin.

Bake for thirty to thirty-five minutes or until the cake is brown on top and springs back when lightly pressed. Cool for five minutes in the tin, then loosen the sides and turn out onto a rack to finish cooling. When cold sift icing sugar evenly over the top.

Apricot jelly with meringues

This is a delicious, strong apricot jelly covered with whipped cream and served with tiny meringues. The jelly can be made well in advance, and can be covered with the cream four or five hours before serving. A piece of plastic wrap lightly dropped over it will keep the cream looking freshly whipped. Of course the meringues can be made in advance too but should not be added to the jelly until just before serving. Will not freeze.

½ lb (225 g) dried apricots
1 pint (570 ml) water
Juice of ½ lemon
¼ pint (150 ml) double
   cream
1 packet orange jelly
Oil for greasing foil

For the meringue:
1 egg white
2 oz (55 g) castor sugar
1 drop vanilla essence

Serves 6

First make the meringue. Set the oven to 100°C/200°F/Gas Mark ½. Whisk the egg white until stiff, then add half the sugar and the vanilla. Whisk again until very stiff and then stir in the remaining 1 oz (30 g) of castor sugar. Put this mixture into a piping bag fitted with a small star nozzle. Lightly oil a large piece of foil and place it on a baking sheet. Pipe the meringue mixture into nut-size meringues. Bake for three-quarters to one-and-a-quarter hours or until the meringues will lift easily off the oiled foil, and are pale biscuit-coloured. Once they are cool store them in an airtight container until needed.

To make the jelly put the dried apricots and a pint of water into a saucepan and bring to the boil. Remove from the heat and allow to soak for an hour. Then return to the heat and cook very gently, covered with a lid, for twenty minutes or until the apricots are soft. With a perforated spoon lift the apricots out of the juice and put them in a blender. Liquidize them to a purée (failing a machine push the fruit through a sieve).

Measure the remaining juice left from cooking the apricots. It should be about ½ pint (290 ml). If it is less, make it up with water. If more, discard some of it. Use this liquid to dissolve the packet of jelly. While it is dissolving measure the liquidized apricot purée and make it up to 1 pint (570 ml) with water. Add the lemon juice. Mix the melted jelly into the apricot purée and pour it into a ring mould or savarin mould.

Dip the mould in hot water and turn the jelly out onto a serving-dish. Whip the cream stiffly and use it to mask the jelly completely. Pile the meringues into the central hole or round the edge, as you prefer. Chill well before serving.

Raspberry Malakoff

Rich and extravagant, I'm afraid, but very simple to make, and irresistible. Will freeze, but it hardly seems worth it when it is so easily prepared.

1 large packet boudoir biscuits or sponge fingers

For the filling:
6 oz (170 g) unsalted butter
6 oz (170 g) castor sugar
6 oz (170 g) ground almonds
½ pint (290 ml) double cream
3 tablespoons Kirsch
½ lb (225 g) fresh raspberries

Oil for greasing paper and dish

Serves 6

The filling can be made in a mixer or with an electric whisk in next to no time. Beat the butter and sugar together until pale in colour and fluffy. Failing a mixer use a wooden spoon and a bowl. Whip the cream until it is stiff but not quite solid. Mix the ground almonds into the sugar and butter mixture, then stir in the Kirsch and finally add the half-whipped cream and the raspberries. Mix thoroughly but avoid beating too hard – the raspberries should as far as possible remain undamaged.

Cut a circle of greaseproof paper to fit the bottom of a straight-sided soufflé dish or cake tin. Brush the paper lightly with oil. Stand the boudoir biscuits up round the edge of the dish with their sugar sides facing outward (that is, against the dish or tin). Spoon the Malakoff mixture into the middle and press down with the back of a wooden spoon or spatula to flatten the top and eliminate any air holes.

Refrigerate overnight or for at least four hours. Using a serrated knife trim the tops of the biscuits so that they come to the same level as the Malakoff filling. Turn the whole pudding out, upside-down, on a serving plate and peel off the oiled greaseproof paper.

Strawberry sorbet

Best results are obtained by using a sorbet-making machine and a deep freeze – ice-boxes in ordinary refrigerators are not really cold enough, though if lowered to their coldest temperature the sorbet will eventually freeze. Chill the serving bowls or glasses well, and serve as promptly as possible. You could pour a spoonful of strawberry liquor over the sorbet when serving. It is a delicious bonanza and prevents the spoon sticking to the tongue if the sorbet is really cold.

¾ lb (340 g) fresh or
    frozen strawberries
6 oz (170 g) castor sugar
½ pint (290 ml) water
1 egg white, stiffly
    whisked
Juice ½ lemon or ½ small
    orange

Serves 4

Bring the water and the sugar to the boil. Boil gently for five minutes. Add the lemon or orange juice. Allow to cool.

Wash the strawberries to remove any sand, and hull them. Liquidize them and stir in the cold syrup.

Place the bowl in the freezer. Stir every twenty minutes. When the mixture is half-frozen whisk the egg white until stiff. Fold it into the strawberry mixture, and return to the freezer. Freeze until solid.

Raspberry sorbet

Serves 4

Proceed as for strawberry sorbet recipe (opposite), but using raspberries instead. Sieve the liquidized fruit if you want to eliminate the raspberry seeds.

Apricot sorbet

14½ oz (410 g) tin apricot halves in syrup
4 fluid oz (110 ml) water
¼ lb (110 g) castor sugar
Juice 1 lemon
Juice 1 orange
2 egg whites

Serves 4

Place the contents of the tin in a liquidizer. Add the sugar, water, and the lemon and orange juices. Liquidize, then pass through a sieve to remove any pieces of skin. Place in the deep freeze, stirring every fifteen minutes until half-frozen. Beat the egg whites until stiff but not dry. Fold them in. Return to the deep freeze until solid.

Prune sorbet

6 oz (170 g) dried prunes
½ pint (290 ml) water
3 oz (85 g) sugar
Juice 1 lemon
Juice 1 orange
2 egg whites

Serves 4

Soak the prunes in the water overnight in a pan, then add the sugar and boil gently for five minutes. Allow to cool. Drain the prunes, keeping the syrup. Remove the prune stones. Liquidize the prunes with the syrup, adding the orange and lemon juices.

Pass through a fine sieve to remove any pieces of skin. Place in the deep freeze, stirring every fifteen minutes until half-frozen. Beat the egg whites well stiff but not dry. Fold them in. Return to the deep freeze until solid.

Orange sorbet

¼ lb (110 g) castor sugar
4 fluid oz (110 ml) water
½ pint (290 ml) fresh orange juice

Serves 4

Dissolve the sugar in the water. Add the orange juice. Taste and add more sugar if necessary. Place the bowl in the deep-freeze and stir regularly every ten to fifteen minutes until fully set.

Hot
Desserts

Baked lemon pudding

This simple family pudding is so delicious I am surprised it does not appear more often. At one point we served it in our restaurant, but so many of our customers, on seeing the risen golden top, expected to find a soufflé before them, and expressed surprise and consternation when they discovered the creamy liquid mixture underneath, that we abandoned it. I had not the courage to risk earning a reputation for making soufflés that separated, and indeed that is what the pudding looks like. Cakey and crisp on top with a lemon curd custard underneath.

2 oz (55 g) butter
¼ lb (110 g) castor sugar
2 medium eggs, separated
¾ oz (20 g) plain flour
Juice and finely grated
    rind of 1 large lemon
½ pint (290 ml) milk
Butter for greasing the
    pie-dish

To serve:
Whipped cream

Serves 4

Butter a 1½ pint (860 ml) soufflé dish or pie-dish. Set the oven to 190°C/375°F/Gas Mark 5.

Cream the butter and sugar together until pale and fluffy, then beat in the egg yolks only. Add the flour, the juice and rind of the lemon, beating well. Mix in the milk, which may well curdle the mixture. But don't worry. Beat the egg whites until stiff but not dry looking and fold them in. Pour the mixture into a soufflé dish or pie-dish and bake for forty-five minutes, by which time the top should be risen and cakey, and golden brown, while the bottom remains a liquid lemon custard. Serve with whipped cream.

St Clement's soufflé

This, as the name implies is an orange and lemon soufflé. To make it successfully night after night in a restaurant can prove tricky. Soufflés need accurate weighing and measuring, and if a chef is busy with a hundred customers' orders soufflé-making may not be something he welcomes. For this reason we experimented with freezing the uncooked soufflé mixture. This works very well, but there are two essential rules. First, the mixture must be frozen the minute the egg whites are folded into it in a good, very cold freezer – the ice compartment of a fridge will not do. In addition, it must be cooked when still absolutely frozen: do not be tempted to allow the soufflé mixture to thaw before cooking. If the soufflé is made in individual ramekin dishes so much the better. With larger dishes there is a danger of having frozen ice-cream in the middle of a hot soufflé mixture. However, many a customer who got this during our experimental period wrote letters asking for the secret of our soufflé surprise with the ice-cream centre!

We are not ashamed to say that occasionally we gild the lily. Try serving cold whipped cream with the soufflés. This is best served in small individual ramekins for each guest. He or she then has a mouthful of hot soufflé with a spoonful of chilled cream. Sacrilege it may be, but it is absolutely delicious.

Put the soufflé into the oven just before eating the main course. This will allow time to eat in peace and even wait a little for the soufflé – remember a soufflé cannot wait, so the guests must.

2 egg yolks
3 egg whites
2 oz (55 g) castor sugar
1½ oz (45 g) plain flour, sieved
8 fluid oz (235 ml) milk
Juice 1 orange
Juice 1 lemon
Finely grated rind of the orange and the lemon

Use the butter to grease a 6-in (15-cm) soufflé dish. Put a spoon of castor sugar in it and tip and turn the dish to ensure that every inch is coated. Gently tap the dish on the work top and tip out all the excess sugar.

Bring the milk to the boil. Heat the oven to 200°C/400°F/Gas Mark 6.

Place the yolks in a mixing bowl, start beating and add three-quarters of the sugar. Beat for two or three minutes until smooth. Slowly add

About ½ oz (15 g) butter, and extra castor sugar for coating the dish
Icing sugar

Serves 4

the flour, stirring thoroughly. Then add the hot milk, still stirring. Return to a pan. Put over the heat and keep stirring well until the mixture thickens, comes to the boil and finally becomes smooth. Add the juices and grated rinds and set aside. Cover tightly to prevent a skin forming.

Now beat the whites of egg until stiff, then fold in the remaining sugar. Fold the whites into the egg custard. Pour into the soufflé dish. Give the dish a sharp tap on the work top to release any over-large bubbles of air that might be trapped in the mixture.

Bake the soufflé on a middle shelf of the oven (with no shelf above it) for twenty-five or thirty minutes until well risen and golden brown. Sprinkle with icing sugar and serve immediately.

Vanderhum soufflé

Follow the instructions for St Clement's soufflé (recipe above) exactly but omit half the orange juice and substitute four tablespoons of Vanderhum liqueur.

Baked banana and rhubarb with burnt sugar

This recipe is very homely and simple, and quite delicious. However, it cannot be done much in advance because the banana is inclined to discolour on keeping.

4 or 5 sticks young pink rhubarb
4 bananas
4 tablespoons brown sugar
2 tablespoons rum (optional)
½ oz (15 g) butter

To serve:
Double cream

Serves 4

Use the butter to grease a shallow oven-proof dish. Cut the bananas in half lengthwise and the rhubarb into sticks about the same length as the bananas. Lay the banana and rhubarb pieces in the dish, alternating them as far as possible. Sprinkle about two tablespoons of the sugar over them and add the rum if liked. Bake the dish, without a lid, in a moderate oven (200°C/400°F/Gas Mark 6) until the rhubarb is cooked through and the bananas are soft (about fifteen to twenty minutes).

Heat the grill well. Sprinkle a further two tablespoons of sugar over the fruit (and a little bit extra if the bananas and rhubarb pieces are large) and brown as quickly as you can under the grill. Serve hot with double cream.

Grand Marnier pancakes

Both pancakes and filling can be prepared in advance. The last-minute grilling of the sugar top will take only a minute or two.

8 French pancakes
  (recipe p. 73)

For the filling:
½ pint (290 ml) milk
2 egg yolks
2 oz (55 g) castor sugar
½ oz (15 g) flour
¾ oz (20 g) cornflour
2 tablespoons double
  cream
Finely grated rind of 1
  orange
3 tablespoons Grand
  Marnier

Icing sugar

Serves 4

First make the pancakes. Next make the custard filling. Put the yolks, sugar and the two flours into a medium-sized heavy saucepan and stir well until smooth. Add ½ pint (290 ml) of milk and the orange rind. Set over medium heat and stir continually while bringing to the boil. The mixture will become alarmingly lumpy but don't panic, just keep stirring steadily. Once the mixture has thickened it will become glossy and smooth. When this stage is reached take the pan off the heat and allow it to cool. Then beat in the double cream and the Grand Marnier.

Use this mixture to fill the French pancakes. Lay them in a heat-proof oven dish and sprinkle them heavily with icing sugar. Get the grill as hot as you can, then put the pancakes under it until the icing sugar has caramelized to a bubbling toffee. Serve at once.

Sweetmeats
&
Petit
Fours

Marzipan log

Few people make their own *friandises* any more because such excellent chocolates and sweetmeats are available commercially. But it is sometimes fun to dip home-grown cherries in caramel, or to make small marzipan sweets for after dinner.

Marzipan (recipe below)
Few drops green
    colouring
Plain chocolate

Work the colouring into the marzipan so that you have a delicately green paste. Roll this into long thin sausage shapes and put them on a wire cake rack. Put the chocolate in the top of a double boiler or on a plate over a pan of simmering water until melted. Using a pastry brush or a spoon coat the marzipan pieces with the chocolate. Once cold and set turn the marzipan strips over and coat the other side with chocolate. Once again allow to cool and harden. Using a sharp knife cut into 1 in (2½ cm) lengths at a slight angle to represent small logs.

Marzipan

1 lb (450 g) ground
    almonds
½ lb (225 g) icing sugar
½ lb (225 g) castor sugar
2 small eggs
Juice of ½ small lemon
Few drops almond essence

If you have a mixing machine put everything together and beat briefly until you have a soft paste. Failing a machine mix the sugars and the almonds together in a bowl, then add the eggs, the lemon juice and the essence and work with your hand to a smooth paste. Wrap well if the marzipan is to be stored.

Coconut cookies

1 lb (450 g) desiccated
    coconut
1 lb (450 g) castor sugar
2 egg whites

Mix everything together in a large heavy saucepan. Put over fairly high heat and stir constantly for ten or twelve minutes. Tip the mixture onto a marble slab or into a large cold bowl and allow it to cool.

Once the mixture is cool enough to handle shape into small balls. Put these out on a baking sheet. Set the oven to 180°C/350°F/Gas Mark 4, and bake until pale brown on top. Allow to cool on the baking tray. Remove them when tepid.

Hazelnut clusters

Shelled hazelnuts
Plain chocolate

Put the hazelnuts into a hot oven and bake for ten minutes or so or until the skins will rub off easily in a tea towel.

Cool the hazelnuts. While they are cooling melt the chocolate in the top of a double boiler or in a soup plate or bowl set over a pan of simmering water. When the chocolate is melted but by no means hot and the nuts are stone-cold coat three or four nuts at a time in chocolate, using two teaspoons. Put the cluster of nuts on oiled greaseproof paper or foil and leave to set and harden.

Fruits dipped in caramel

Cherries, grapes, segments of orange or fresh mandarins are good dipped in candied sugar. They must be absolutely dry and undamaged before dipping. If the fruit must be washed, do this the day before dipping and allow to dry completely. They cannot be dipped more than two or three hours in advance, and must be stored somewhere dry and cool before serving – a steamy kitchen will quickly make them sticky.

Melt granulated sugar in a heavy saucepan, then allow it to bubble to a pale toffee. Remove immediately from the heat. Dip the fruit (holding it with tongs or tweezers if you prefer), one piece at a time, into the caramel. Set the dipped fruits on oiled foil until the sugar has hardened. Then transfer them to paper cases, or the serving-dish.

After-dinner brandy snaps

Follow the recipe on page 160 for brandy snaps but making only half the quantity and putting the mixture out in the smallest possible teaspoons – a coffeespoon would be ideal. When cooked (they will probably take less than four minutes) bend them round an oiled pencil or the handle of a small wooden spoon. Do not fill them. Once cold store in an airtight container.

Menu
Suggestions

January	Artichoke and leek soup
	Halibut steaks with prawns, mushrooms and lemon butter
	Pears in crême de menthe
	Avocadoes with apple and crab
	Leith's duckling
	Classic chocolate mousse
February	Taramasalata and pitta bread
	Grilled spicy spring chicken with oriental rice
	Bourdaloue tart with apricots
	Hot spinach with mushrooms
	Rack of lamb with parsley and garlic
	Italian meringue pie
March	Seafood kebab with tarragon sauce
	Chicken casseroled in claret
	Passionfruit syllabub
	Smoked trout paté
	Breast of chicken in puff pastry, Madeira sauce
	Prune sorbet
April	Tomatoes filled with ham and cottage cheese
	Seatrout in a foil case
	Almond pastry fruit flan
	Crab bisque
	Spring lamb with bacon and kidney
	Lemon mousse
May	Deep fried Gruyère and chicken pancakes
	Poached trout with cream and fennel sauce
	Figs and pears in orange juice
	Stuffed eggs with cheese and tomatoes
	Garlic lamb steak
	Profiteroles with cream and apricot sauce
June	Cucumber and mushroom salad
	Lemon sole fillets stuffed with salmon and herb mousse
	Beignets with apricot sauce
	Squid and prawn salad
	Quails in pastry
	Vanilla ice-cream with passionfruit

July	Green mayonnaise eggs
	Salmon quenelles with Chablis cream sauce
	Greek fruit salad with ice

July
: Green mayonnaise eggs
: Salmon quenelles with Chablis cream sauce
: Greek fruit salad with ice

: Cucumber with yoghurt and mint
: Veal in a mild curry sauce with fresh pineapple
: Strawberry ring

August
: Melon filled with prawns and celery
: Fillet steak with green peppercorn sauce
: Raspberry sorbet

: Leith's gazpacho
: Seafood vol-au-vents
: Damson ice-cream

September
: Baked egg with sorrel
: Roast grouse with cranberries, bread sauce, breadcrumbs
: Vacherin with grapes and chestnuts

: Scallops with chorizo
: Sweetbreads in cream and calvados
: Almond cake

October
: Lentil and bacon soup
: Grilled mackerel with mustard sauce
: Pears in burgundy

: Moules marinières
: Fillet of beef in pastry with mushroom stuffing
: Pistachio ice-cream

November
: Celeriac remoulade
: Stuffed breast of turkey, port wine sauce
: Peppermint pears

: Mackerel fillets Provençale
: Braised oxtail with flageolets
: Baked banana and rhubarb with burnt sugar

December
: Baked gnocchi
: Pheasant casserole with chestnuts
: Ginger cream

: Leith's Stilton soup
: Mr Reynaud's juniper hare
: Orange sorbet

Index